M000120235

The Principle of
Effect and Cause

Any mistakes we made in the past are insignificant compared with the future we are going to create from here on. The past is merely a process through which we have reached this point in time. Now that we are here in this moment, we no longer need the past. All we need to do is to look toward the future.

The

PRINCIPLE

of

Effect

and

Cause

Changing the Future by
Changing Our Way of Thinking

MASAMI SAIONJI

© Masami Saionji 2019
All rights reserved.

ISBN-13: 978-1-0733-7938-5
ISBN-10: 1-0733-7938-8

Translated by Kinuko Hamaya and David W. Edelstein
Edited by Mary L. McQuaid

Cover and book design by David W. Edelstein
Cover and interior illustration elements by Freepik.com

Contents

Appendices

The law of cause and effect—also known as karma—
says that we must inevitably reap the consequences
of the seeds we have sown (our thoughts, words, and
actions from past and present lifetimes). To transcend
this law of cause and effect, I have put forth the
principle of *effect and cause.*

According to this principle, when we depict in our
mind and with our words the circumstances that we
desire, we inscribe those circumstances in the future.
In doing so, we draw forth in this present-day world
the causes that lead to those future results, so that in
time, we are able to bring about the future we desire.

The Principle of Effect and Cause

Consciousness transformation in the 21st century

Vision for a peaceful society

*D*uring the 20th century, we tried various measures in our quest to create a peaceful society on earth and bring ourselves happiness—we tried to do away with war, poverty, and hunger, we distributed food, we provided training in science and technology, we made advances in the fields of politics and economics, we tried to prevent the destruction of nature, and so on. A great many leaders and specialists made all kinds of efforts to work out the best possible measures in their respective fields. However, none of these measures brought true peace or happiness to humanity. What is the reason for this? I believe it is because those measures only addressed the symptoms of society's ills, without deeply considering their source.

Now, humanity needs a more fundamental solution. That is to say, we need a transformation in consciousness. This is because, no matter how many times we may avert wars or hold back the destruction of nature, if humanity does not make a fundamental change in its consciousness, the same conditions will surface over and over again.

On the other hand, if we human beings are able to change our consciousness and accept all the things that happen in our lives in a positive way, then war, poverty, hunger, and natural destruction will cease to occur. Everything will naturally be guided to a state of harmony, and a peaceful society will be built.

At present, however, a great many people are still caught up in negative thought-habits. Here, let us look at some examples of negative and positive thought-habits that people have developed:

Half my life is gone! vs. *I still have half my life in front of me.*
I am too old to do that vs. *There are lots of things I can still do.*
These are the last days of my life vs. *This is the first day of the*

rest of my life.
I cannot move my legs vs. *I can still move my hands.*

Each example gives us two ways of expressing the very same situation. One represents dark, negative thinking, while the other expresses a bright, positive way of thinking. Which of these patterns do you usually fall into? If all your thoughts are dark and negative, you are most likely leading a gloomy, suffocating life, without nurturing any bright hopes. Indeed, many, many people on our planet are living this way at present.

Why do so many of us end up thinking negatively? Perhaps it is because, deep in our minds, we harbor all sorts of fears and anxieties about the future. The most prominent of these is the fear of death. *When will I die? How will I die? I don't want to die!* It would not be an overstatement to say that, consciously or unconsciously, many of us are constantly plagued by thoughts like these.

The next most common fear that we hold is fear regarding our relationships. Living in society requires us to maintain relationships—with our spouse or partner, our parents, our children, our brothers and sisters, our friends, acquaintances, neighbors, relatives, and co-workers. And so, from a very young age, we attach considerable importance to our relationships with others. Sometimes we may doubt ourselves, thinking, *Will my friends leave me or turn against me? Will they stop caring about me when they see my faults?*

On top of these, we live with all kinds of other fears—fear of getting sick, fear of getting old, fear of being unhappy, fear of being poor, and fear of losing our social status, our reputation, and our family bonds. Most of the time, we try to suppress these fears, leaving them locked away deep in our mind. But occasionally, they suddenly rise to the surface, and the thing we have long feared manifests in our reality.

Fears and anxieties connected with the law of cause and effect

Why are we living with so much fear? I think it is because we cannot see our future—we have no idea what will happen, or when. Furthermore, we are convinced that someday, we will have to accept the consequences of things we did in the past. We think this way because we believe in the law of cause and effect—that a particular cause leads to a particular effect. I think many people are already familiar with this law, but the general principle is that everything occurs as the result of a cause, and if there is no cause, nothing will take place.

Because the couple fell in love, they married. Because the wife was busy with her job, they did not see much of each other. Because they did not see much of each other, the husband turned to someone else for love and affection. Because the husband was unfaithful, the marriage ended in divorce. In these examples, we recognize certain causes as producing certain effects.

All the various circumstances in the world can be explained through this law of cause and effect. Under this law there is first a cause, and then an effect. A seed that was sown in the past will eventually bring forth some result. Most of us today are living in fear of a future we cannot see, wondering when that effect will reveal itself in our life.

When we are living in fear, we tend to focus on our shortcomings, lack confidence in ourselves, feel inferior to others, and fall into negative ways of thinking. Often, through the power of our thoughts, our excessive fear of undesirable circumstances ends up drawing those very circumstances right to us. We forget that something perfect dwells within every one of us—that each of us is furnished with wisdom, ability, beauty, intuition, potential, and infinitely more. How much brighter our lives would be if, instead of pouring energy into struggling against our shortcomings, we worked on making the most of our strengths! Let's take another look at the examples I gave earlier:

Half my life is gone! vs. *I still have half my life in front of me.*
I am too old to do that vs. *There are lots of things I can still do.*
These are the last days of my life vs. *This is the first day of the rest of my life.*
I cannot move my legs vs. *I can still move my hands.*

As these examples suggest, the way we perceive our present and future circumstances has a decisive influence on the direction our life will take. If we always believe in the positive, we activate our hidden potential and open up new, brightly lit avenues to the future. On the other hand, if we get caught up in the things we have lost and the negative sides of ourselves, we end up attracting unnecessary, unpleasant experiences and mishaps, and we repeat these unwanted experiences again and again.

For many long years, humanity has continued giving energy to its fears and anxieties, turning them into realities. Because of this, we have come to see all the phenomena that occur in our lives in terms of the law of cause and effect. We have accepted this law as a matter of course, never doubting it for a moment, and we have continually let it control our lives.

However, during the 21st century, we human beings will be able to make a shift from the law of cause and effect to the principle of *effect and cause*. And, as each of us begins to grasp this principle and put it into practice, we will be able to discover true happiness. This is because the principle of *effect and cause* enables us to draw out our inner radiance and our innate faculties and energy, and in doing so, create a future that is filled with hope. When we live according to this principle, we can use it as a method for transcending the old law of cause and effect. Once we fully understand it, it becomes completely unnecessary for us to concern ourselves with the past. As a result, we can remake our present and future in whatever ways we like.

Which comes first, the cause or the effect?

If only I had more money, I could have a nicer home, we might think. *If I could always be with the person I love, I would not be lonely at all.* In these examples, the causes are 'having more money' and 'always being with the one

I love,' and the effects are 'having a nicer home' and 'not being lonely.' With the law of cause and effect, the cause always comes first, and the effect always follows. After that, the effect turns into a new cause.

On the other hand, with the principle of *effect and cause*, the effect always comes first. This effect is not rooted in a pre-existing cause; rather, it springs from the world of infinite potential that resides within each and every human being.

With the law of cause and effect, the primary cause is always something finite. *If I had money*, or *if I could always be with a certain person*—conditions like these depend on the circumstances in the material world, so they cannot last forever. On the other hand, under the principle of *effect and cause*, the effect is always based on something that is changeless and unlimited. Infinite love, infinite health, infinite richness, infinite life—when we turn our attention to these limitless qualities that spring from the realm of the spirit, they spontaneously generate all sorts of marvelous new causes.

To live by the principle of *effect and cause*, the first thing we need to do is to recognize that, if we truly desire, from the bottom of our heart, to do something or to become something, the ability to achieve our desire

is already present within us. Once we reach this understanding, all our thought-habits can shift to a more elevated dimension.

From future to present to past

The next difference I would like to point out is the way
in which these two approaches view time. In the law of
cause and effect, everything flows from past to present to
future, while in the principle of *effect and cause*, it flows in
the other direction—from future to present to past.

The law of cause and effect tells us that what happens
in the present is determined by a cause generated in the
past. That is, the overall flow is from past to present. For
example, we might view our present illness as the result
of a series of events linking back to a single cause in the
past, thinking: *Because of everything that happened in the
past, it was determined that I would contract this illness.*
This present illness then becomes a new cause, and as
the flow continues from present to future, it generates a
future outcome. This is how time is viewed in the law of
cause and effect.

With this way of thinking, we have no present or future means to do anything about this illness. All we can

do is to silently accept our fate. This is because both our present and future are seen as the unavoidable consequences of our past. If we had made a different choice in the past, we might have been able to avoid the illness, but since we cannot go back and change what happened, we think that we cannot change the present, either. And if the present cannot be changed, neither can the future. This is to say that, under the law of cause and effect, we live as prisoners of the past, without any free will at all.

However, with the principle of *effect and cause*, our flow moves from future to present, and the starting point is when we ourselves create our own future 'result.' Let's take the example of a river—it flows from upstream to downstream. Suppose you are standing in the river, and you pick up a leaf that has fallen near you and write your present hope or dream on that leaf. Then, you throw the leaf into the water. If you throw the leaf downstream, your hope or dream will never make its way back to you. The moment it leaves your hand, it quickly flows down the river—in other words, into the past.

When you throw the leaf, you must be sure to throw it upstream, by imagining your vision and hope for the future. When you send your wish upstream—into the future—it will gradually flow down from there. And now, that leaf of hope that left your hand days, months, or years ago is finally passing in front of you. If you catch hold of it, the thing that you wished for will become a reality.

Under this principle, time flows from the future to the present. Therefore, if we take every opportunity, every single day, to throw leaves of hope—tens, hundreds, thousands of leaves—into the future, some of these leaves are sure to appear before us and come true. If we take this present moment to clearly depict in our mind the hopes and plans that will make our life ever more radiant—if we repeat to ourselves over and over, *It's absolutely all right! I can definitely do it! Everything is possible! Everything is perfect! Everything has been perfectly accomplished!*—our positive words and thoughts will indeed manifest in our life.

Because our life flows from the future to the present, and from the present to the past, the things that we think and say over and over again about the future will eventually make their way to the present and come true. As we keep sending forth our future hopes and dreams again and again, one by one, they will flow down to the present, and the moment will surely come when we can catch hold of these leaves—the hope-filled visions that we threw into the future. This is the principle of *effect and cause*.

Up to now, most of us have been working to improve our lives by identifying the causes generated in the past, digging up the unwanted seeds one by one and getting rid of them. With this method, it was very difficult to achieve our goals, because our consciousness was focused on what was downstream—the negative causes from the past. But when we change our way of thinking to the principle of *effect and cause*, elevating our consciousness by looking toward the future (upstream) without being bound by or lamenting what happened in the past, we awaken the wonderful qualities that reside within us, and turn our lives in a better direction.

A wonderful example

I would like to share with you a story that serves as a perfect example of the principle of *effect and cause*. In 2011, I went to France to attend a UNESCO general forum. An acquaintance of mine who lives there came to help me as a volunteer. At that time, she told me about her experience.

Hers is a success story in which she overcame her illness by means of her elevated consciousness, her unwavering self-belief, and her invincible sense of purpose.

Her story serves as proof that no matter who we are, our physical body is endowed with a wonderful, infinite power to naturally heal itself.

This woman fell ill one day, and she became bed-ridden and unable to walk. Of course, she consulted doctors, but since the cause of her illness could not be clearly identified, they were unable to treat her for it. However, since she was young, this woman believed in the body's natural healing power, and so she resolved to heal herself on her own.

At first, it was painfully difficult just to turn over in bed. Nevertheless, she took it as the perfect chance to put the principle of *effect and cause* into practice. In her mind, she envisioned her hope for the future, and she compelled herself to keep trying and keep looking forward. Every day was a battle with herself—a series of painful ordeals. But no matter how much pain and difficulty she endured, she never gave up, and she hardly ever had a negative thought. Instead, she continued to focus on the positive and apply the principle of *effect and cause*, thinking: *I will never give up. I will not surrender. Everything is sure to get better. Everything is absolutely all right. Everything has been perfectly accomplished!*

First, she depicted in her mind an overall image of

her healthy self—the accomplishment of her hope and dream. Then, she focused on the small steps that lay before her, and one by one, made each of them a reality.

She started with turning over in bed, but even this first step was already quite an ordeal. When she just moved her body slightly—let alone rolled over—intense pain would course through her entire body, to the point of making her scream. Despite this, she never gave up. Little by little, with both body and mind, she kept striving and persevering toward her goal. She kept up her positive way of thinking, and finally, she was able to turn over. The first step toward her dream was accomplished.

The next challenge was to get up from her bed. Giving it all the strength she had, she stood up and fell back down again and again, until finally, she was able to stand up. The next step was to walk to the bathroom by herself. It took tremendous time and effort just to put her foot forward. But she took her time, focusing on taking one step at a time, completely absorbed in the act of walking, and eventually she accomplished this task as well. Then, her challenge was to leave the house and walk outside on her own. She kept up her training, never slackening her efforts for a moment, and as a result, she finally made it out her front door. She had accomplished this goal as well.

The very last—and greatest—step was to walk from her house to a nearby telephone pole. She told me that this was truly an immense undertaking. What might take another person only five minutes took her about an hour. But having come this far, rising to each challenge step by step, she had built up confidence in herself, and finally was able to make the principle of *effect and cause* her own. It became her habit, she said, and gradually was easier to put into practice.

In tears, she told me that she had taken a train and come to the UNESCO headquarters by herself—the first time since falling ill that she had done such a thing. She had a noble consciousness, her radiant smile was truly beautiful, she was filled with self-confidence, and her words and actions exhibited a marvelous sense of dignity. Everything she said was a great lesson to me, and I expressed my deepest gratitude to her. What an amazing person! What incredible self-belief! I wondered if I myself would be able to do what she did.

She put the principle of *effect and cause* into practice, and proved how effective it is. She affirmed that just by shifting from a negative to a positive way of thinking, she was able to transform despair into bright hopes for the future.

Keep your consciousness turned in a bright direction

If every phenomenon and result that reveals itself in our life plunges us into despair, leading us to thoughts like, *I can't do this anymore*, *It's too difficult*, *It's too troublesome*, and *I can't bear it*, then we will not be able to accomplish anything. The more these feelings pile up, the closer we come to giving up altogether.

But if, as in the principle of *effect and cause*, we hold up bright, shining visions like, *I can definitely do this! I am shining radiantly!* and *Every day I feel happier and happier!* and if we keep making efforts toward our goals, we will surely be able to achieve them, just like my friend who was able to turn over in bed and walk on her own. Then, the independent spirit and true joy that comes from these accomplishments—from knowing that we are guiding ourselves—will lift us up to new heights.

In this way, our consciousness works freely, just as we desire. It knows no bounds. For this reason, it is vital that we always direct our consciousness toward harmony and toward the positive.

When we fix our attention on the law of cause and effect and fret over how we can take responsibility for the seeds that we planted in the past, we end up getting dragged into and fixated on those past causes, and we blame ourselves, judge ourselves, and repudiate ourselves. With this kind of dark, negative thinking, we are unable to see any light at all.

In contrast, with the principle of *effect and cause*, even if our past causes lead to unpleasant effects, we continue to look at everything in a bright, positive way. We focus our consciousness on the future, thinking, *When this passes, everything will definitely get better. Everything will be all right.* When we take this approach, no negative thoughts need ever enter our mind.

Up to now, most of us have been too caught up with things that happened in the past. Looking back at the past from the point in time called 'now,' we passively dread the day when the things we did in the past will bear their results. But instead of thinking this way, we can look ahead toward the future and actively seize the opportunity to change our life, thinking, *The future that I am steadily creating will someday manifest in my life.* If we hold a bright thought in our mind now, we will experience it at some point in the future.

Any mistakes we made in the past are insignificant compared with the future we are going to create from here on. The past is merely a process through which we have reached this point in time. Now that we are here in this moment, we no longer need the past. All we need to do is to look toward the future.

Taking the initiative to create a new future

Each and every one of us has been given the freedom to choose. What kind of life are we choosing to live? Are we choosing to think, '*I am controlled by my past,*' or are we choosing to think, '*Right now, I am creating a new future*'? Are we choosing to think, '*Half my life is gone,* or *I still have half my life in front of me*'?

If we have been holding on to self-restrictive, fixed ideas, now is the time to change those fixed ideas. Let us take the initiative in creating a new future for ourselves and for humanity with the principle of *effect and cause*. In the 21st century, each and every human being will live in the world that they themselves envision and create. This world need not be the negative world that we have seen throughout history. It can be a brightly shining world of freedom and bliss.

The principle of *effect and cause* tells us that if we wish to be happier, the first thing to do is to envision and believe in our already happy self. Instead of thinking, *I want to be happy*, we believe that happiness has already been achieved, thinking, *I am happy!* If we think, *I want to be happy*, we are acknowledging that we are not happy now. Whatever our present situation may be, and whatever might have happened in our past, we need to do away with the old fixed ideas we have held up to now and replace them with an entirely new, light-filled consciousness. We need to start by catching hold of a radiant future outcome.

The principle of *effect and cause* is not simply a matter of will power. It is a matter of focusing our mind on our wonderful innate abilities, in order to draw forth the limitless potential for happiness that resides innately within us. Living by this principle does not take happiness away from others, and therefore, it leaves no one unhappy.

When we focus on our innate ability to be happy, we can affirm to ourselves: *I am happy. With all my heart, I love myself and believe in myself. I am using the abilities I have been given to create a radiant future. I am living my life in a way that is helpful to others.* Once we have transformed our consciousness in this way, all the conditions that we wish for will be arranged and will gradually take shape in our life. As we continue to maintain this consciousness, eventually we will arrive at the very future that we have envisioned. It will become a reality. This is because consciousness is energy—the very energy that gives shape to this world.

The principle of *effect and cause* starts with believing in ourselves, and believing that all human beings— ourselves included—are, by nature, good-hearted and well-intentioned. By affirming our faith in human nature, we are able to create a brightly shining future for humanity.

We need to show greater respect for our own lives. We need to have absolute authority over our own existence. When we know deep in our being that human nature is essentially good, for the first time, we become able to forgive ourselves. And when we can truly forgive ourselves, we naturally become able to forgive others, as well.

In order to continue radiantly evolving and creating ourselves throughout the course of our lives, it is vital that we honestly accept ourselves for who we are—no matter who we are—and that we strive to live according to the principle of *effect and cause*. The marvelous, shining person within us loves and respects all humanity, and is helping to guide the world toward peace.

During the 21st century, as more and more human beings transform their consciousness and live by the principle of *effect and cause*, we will move away from a future filled with anxieties and toward a future of spiritual peace and stability.

Originally published in Japanese, April 2012

All Wisdom Is Woven into Your Genes

Something most important as we live

Everything we need to carry out our entire lifetime is already woven into our genes. Artistic talent, wisdom, good health, prosperity, good fortune, and many other amazing qualities and faculties are explicitly programmed into each and every cell of our bodies. As we live in this world, understanding this truth is the most important and most valuable thing each of us can do.

From the moment of our birth, everything we desire, hope for, and aspire to is already part of us. It is by drawing forth our innate wisdom, health, talent, ability, and all our wonderful qualities during the course of our life and demonstrating them in this world that we are able to lead a dynamic, fulfilling life. These resources cannot be found by searching outside ourselves, nor can anyone give them to us. They cannot be received from God or from heaven, either. They already exist within us, clearly inscribed in our genes.

The extent to which we are able to draw out these innate qualities during our life will determine the course of our future. Success or failure, prosperity or decline, health or illness, happiness or unhappiness—all of these phenomena are brought about through our own past words, thoughts, and actions, and we cannot curse or blame anyone else for them. I say this because if some undesirable condition or circumstance—some misfortune, illness, loneliness, or distress—is taking place in our life, it is either because we have not yet drawn forth all of our genetically inscribed abilities, or because we have not fully recognized and grasped that such almighty wisdom does indeed reside within us.

Look at the flowers blooming in a field, or at animals frolicking in nature. Just like us, before they were born in this world, they inherited a set of genes from their parents, and they are dutifully living out the lives inscribed in those genes, carrying out their own divinely given missions. With their inborn instincts, they are living as part of the world of nature. Displaying blooms of myriad colors that wave in the breeze, the flowers live out their lives entrusting themselves to nature. If the flowers are red, then the instruction to make red pigment is inscribed in the plant's genes.

Look at a flock of birds dancing in the sky. As they stretch out their resplendent wings and fly smoothly through the sky, notice their form, their colors, the way they fly, and the way they catch their food. They do not learn any of these things from anyone. They are simply demonstrating the natural way of life that is programmed in their genes. When a butterfly lays an egg, the egg turns into a larva, the larva turns into a chrysalis, and finally into a new butterfly. Truly magnificent functions are at work throughout this one lifetime, all of which are inscribed in the butterfly's genes.

These plants and animals do not need to make difficult decisions or tax their brains more than necessary. With little or no effort, they simply merge with the world of nature and become part of it, living within nature as nature sustains their lives.

However, when it comes to human beings, things are not so simple. Unlike the animals, plants, minerals, and other things that exist as part of nature, we human beings are not living naturally. Instead, we go out of our way to make everything in our lives complex and elaborate. In most cases, our knowledge races on ahead and our bodies cannot catch up. All of us have within us marvelous faculties and sensibilities, such as our intuition, sense of beauty, and the ability to take action in response to danger or a poisonous substance. If we entrust ourselves to our natural instincts and needs, we can go through life naturally, with no feeling of distress or failure. But because we make judgments based on our imperfect knowledge and past experience, we go against nature and our intuition, dull our instinctive reactions, and guide ourselves in unexpected directions. As a result, we end up driving ourselves down paths of uncertainty and unhappiness.

Here, I would like to reaffirm that all wisdom and all power and ability are already woven into our genes. I am not talking about the genes of special people, such as Nobel Prize winners. The genes of great scientists, statesmen, business leaders, and artists are not special. It is just that these people recognized the talents that already resided within them and manifested them in this world. There is no difference at all between the genes of these outstanding people and the genes of ordinary people like us. All that differentiates us is whether or not we are cognizant of the wisdom inscribed in our genes, and the extent to which we can actually draw it out and make use of it in our lives. Those who became great scientists and artists are people who perceived and understood their innate talents, and endeavored to draw them out from inside.

Meanwhile, most people today are living unaware that all wisdom already exists within them, and are convinced that there is nothing more to them than the physical body they can see and touch. No matter how hard and how patiently they toil away, again and again, their lives fail to meet their ideals. My advice to such people is to give recognition to all the wisdom that is dormant within them, and to wake it up! This is the best way to break out of whatever difficult circumstances and conditions we now face.

Awaken to your inner wisdom

It is mistaken to think that you have no talent. Unrivalled talent in every field is already woven into your genes.

It is mistaken to think that you have no sense of beauty.

An exquisite sense of beauty is already woven into your genes.

It is mistaken to think that you have a poor memory. Your genes are already furnished with the power to absorb everything into memory.

It is mistaken to think that you have no artistic sensibility. Delicate artistic abilities are already hidden in your genes.

It is mistaken to think that you have no faculty for science and mathematics. A talent for precise scientific and mathematical work is woven into your genes.

It is mistaken to think that you have no faculty for the humanities. A natural gift for understanding the humanities is woven into your genes.

It is mistaken to think that you have dull reflexes and poor coordination. Marvelous athletic abilities are already woven into your genes.

It is mistaken to think that you cannot maintain your health. A strong natural healing power is already woven into your genes.

In this way, great divine wisdom is inscribed in each and every one of the billions and trillions of cells that comprise our present physical body. It is important to be aware of this truth, as it is a shame to leave this wisdom untouched. We are doing ourselves a great disservice by not awakening and activating it. Each of us—every one of the seven billion human beings on earth—needs to open our eyes to this wonderful and amazing truth as soon as possible. It is this understanding that lets us lead meaningful lives and accomplish our missions, so that we are not just wandering through life in a miserable state.

Despite the truth that such marvelous, infinite abilities are woven right into each of our genes, we have looked right past them, without ever taking notice. Yet, it is never too late. Our physical body is such a wondrous, sublime, intricate entity, we cannot operate or re-create any part of it, no matter how hard we exert our knowledge and power. Keeping all our internal organs working, maintaining a consistent blood density, extracting nutrition from the food we eat and excreting the waste materials—we cannot reproduce or control even one of these functions with our own knowledge and power. In reality, we have no choice but to entrust everything about our body to our internal functions.

What is it that sustains and operates these internal functions—a task which even the full use of our knowledge and ability cannot accomplish? It is the life-power that dwells within each of us—a power that activates, harmonizes, and operates everything that goes on inside our body. The sooner we give honest recognition to this power, the sooner we will be able to lead a more abundant and more fulfilling life.

Just think—all of this power, ability, and wisdom have been hidden deep inside us. How inspiring this is, and how thankful it makes us feel! And at the same time, how senseless it seems that, up to now, we have been suffering pain and hardship without awakening to this truth.

We are living in a world where few people understand the reality of their own uniquely wonderful existence, and everyone tries to follow the same path through life. We are tracing the same path that was laid out for us by others who went before, without trying to improve it—without even doubting or questioning it. Placing high regard on morals and doctrines, and holding fast to commonly-held ideas and assumptions, we are doing our utmost to pursue this established path. It is a way of life that compels us to search for God outside ourselves, to seek success from outside ourselves, and to pursue happiness outside ourselves.

However, we are going about it all the wrong way.

God resides not only outside us, but within us as well. Success and prosperity reside within us. Happiness already exists within us. How did we make such a mistake? Where did we go wrong?

Up to now, the forces that move this world have been based in misunderstandings and illusions. Genuine understanding has remained far distant, and has yet to firmly take root in the world and in each of our minds. Everything has been a product of our misunderstandings and illusions, which have gone unchallenged and unnoticed, and we have accepted much of what happens in this world as a matter of course. And so, no matter how many times saints, sages, and great pioneers introduce true teachings into this world, it will never bring about any change as long as the majority of people are lost in a world of misunderstanding and illusion, a world where truth is distorted.

The Necklace by Maupassant

Speaking of misunderstandings, I am reminded of a short story that I read many years ago—a story called *The Necklace* by Guy de Maupassant. Here, I would like to include an abridged version that conveys the gist of the story:

She was one of those pretty and charming girls born, as though fate had blundered over her, into a family of workers. She had no marriage portion, no expectations, no means of getting known, understood, loved, and wedded by a man of wealth and distinction; and she let herself be married off to a little clerk in the Ministry of Education.

Her tastes were simple because she had never been able to afford any other. She suffered endlessly, feeling herself born for every delicacy and luxury. She suffered from the poorness of her house, from its mean walls, worn chairs, and ugly curtains. All these things, of which other women of her class would not even have been aware, tormented and insulted her.

She had no clothes, no jewels, nothing. And these were the only things she loved; she felt that she was made for them. She had longed so eagerly to charm, to be desired, to be wildly attractive and sought after.

One evening her husband came home with an exultant air, holding a large envelope in his hand. It was an invitation to a party to be held at the residence of the Minister of Education. Instead of being delighted, as her husband hoped, she flung the invitation petulantly across the table, murmuring:

"What do you want me to do with this? And what do you suppose I am to wear at such an affair? I haven't a dress and so I can't go to this party."

He was at a loss. Nevertheless, he wanted to please his wife, so he used all the money he had saved to buy her a new dress. The day of the party drew near, and the wife, who had been happy at first, seemed sad, uneasy and anxious. Her husband asked her why.

"I'm utterly miserable at not having any jewels, not a single stone, to wear," she replied. "I shall look absolutely no one. I would almost rather not go to the party."

"Wear flowers," he said. "They're very smart at this time of the year. For ten francs you could get two or three gorgeous roses." She was not convinced.

After pondering it over, her husband came upon the idea of his wife borrowing jewels from her rich friend. Next day she went to see her friend and told her her trouble. Madame Forestier went to her dressing-table, took up a large box, brought it to Madame Loisel, opened it, and said: "Choose, my dear."

First she saw some bracelets, then a pearl necklace, then a Venetian cross in gold and gems, of exquisite workmanship. Then, she saw a superb diamond necklace, and chose that.

The day of the party arrived. Madame Loisel was a success. She was the prettiest woman present, elegant, graceful, smiling, and quite above herself with happiness. All the men stared at her, inquired her name, and asked to be introduced to her.

All the Under-Secretaries of State were eager to waltz with her. The Minister noticed her.

She danced madly, ecstatically, drunk with pleasure, with no thought for anything, in the triumph of her beauty, in the pride of her success, in a cloud of happiness made up of this universal homage and admiration, of the desires she had aroused, of the completeness of a victory so dear to her feminine heart.

After returning home, she discovered that the necklace was no longer round her neck! She and her husband were horrified. They searched all her clothing and over all the ground they had walked, but they could not find it.

Then they went from jeweller to jeweller, searching for another necklace like the first. Finally, they found a string of diamonds which seemed to them exactly like the one they were looking for. It was worth thirty-six thousand francs.

To borrow the money, her husband gave notes of hand, entered into ruinous agreements, did business with usurers and the whole tribe of money-lenders. He mortgaged the whole remaining years of his existence, appalled at the agonising face of the future, at the black misery about to fall upon him.

When Madame Loisel took back the necklace to Madame Forestier, the latter said to her: "You ought to have brought it back sooner; I might have needed it." But she did not notice the substitution.

They changed their flat; they took a garret under the roof. She came to know the heavy work of the house, the hateful duties of the kitchen that wore out her beautiful skin and nails. And, clad like a poor woman, she went to the fruiterer, to the grocer, to the butcher, a basket on her arm, haggling, insulted, fighting for every wretched halfpenny of her money.

This life lasted ten years. At the end of ten years everything was paid off, everything, the usurer's charges and the accumulation of superimposed interest.

Madame Loisel looked old now. She had become like all the other strong, hard, coarse women of poor households. Her hair was badly done, her skirts were awry, her hands were red.

One Sunday, as she had gone for a walk along the Champs-Élysées, she caught sight suddenly of a woman who was taking a child out for a walk. It was her rich friend, Madame Forestier.

She went up to her, but as she had completely lost the beautiful looks she once had, the other at first did not recognize her. Then, she uttered a cry: "Oh! ... my poor Mathilde, how you have changed! ..."

Since all the debts had been paid off, she told her friend everything that had happened.

"You say you bought a diamond necklace to replace mine?"

her friend replied. "Oh, my poor Mathilde! But mine was imitation. It was worth at the very most five hundred francs! ..." [1]

The perils of misunderstanding and illusion

I think that Maupassant's intention with this story was to depict, to the fullest extent, the ugliness and odiousness of the vanity and ostentation that were lurking in Madame Loisel's mind. If she had been gratefully content with the new dress that her poor husband had bought for her, she wouldn't have had to lead such a wretched and unbearably miserable life. But she wanted more than just the dress—she wanted jewels to make her look even more beautiful. From that moment on, the couple's life together took a totally unexpected turn for the worse.

In the past, I understood the story as an expression of the weakness that lurks in all of our hearts, as well as the immensely destructive power of vanity. However, the way I feel about it now is a little different. The main theme I glean from this work is the misunderstanding and illusion that any of us can easily fall into.

When Madame Loisel's rich friend took out her jewelry and told Madame Loisel that she could take whichever piece she liked, she picked the diamond necklace. At that time, she could never have imagined that her rich friend would show her imitation jewelry. Her belief that they were genuine was a misunderstanding and an illusion. Indeed, many unfortunate incidents are brought about in this world because we are utterly misguided in what we see, hear, feel, and believe. I suppose everyone reading this has had one or two such experiences, where you made a mistake, hurt someone's feelings, or had your feelings hurt by someone due to some misunderstanding or illusory thinking.

A mirage is another kind of illusion. It is a phenomenon where excessive heat and cold in the atmosphere cause light to refract in unusual ways, making it look like there is something in the air or on the ground that isn't really there. It is said that travelers who walk through the scorching desert for many days are often deceived by mirages. They think that, for example, there is a lake just ahead where they can get a drink of water. However, although the mirage they saw in the distance was so clear, when they reach the spot, they find no trace of the lake. The image looked so real that the travelers were convinced it was really there.

Just like these travelers, we are wasting our precious lives for the sake of misunderstandings and illusions.

Without making any effort to see the radiant wisdom and abilities that already dwell inside us, we believe that the things we desire exist outside of us, somewhere far away. And just as desert travelers chase after mirages, we are chasing after this illusory happiness. So much of what we think and do is based in illusion. The illusion that our unhappiness and distress can be relieved by something outside of us. The illusion that an external God will grant our wishes, heal our illnesses, and give us anything we ask for. The illusion that all of the misfortunes, disasters, pain, and sorrow we experience are not our own responsibility, but the fault of someone else.

And there are many more. The illusion that honor, fame, money, and power are something absolute in this world, the illusion that we are not a first-rate person unless we graduate from a first-rate school, and the illusion that all clergymen, people of holy orders, and others who serve God are pure and splendid individuals—just to name a few. We are compelled by everything around us to lead lives beset with all kinds of misunderstandings and illusions. Until all of humanity awaken from these illusions and see things as they truly are, this way of living will continue on, passed down to our children, our grandchildren, and our great-grandchildren.

Trusting and loving ourselves

Here, I would like to ask you the following questions:

> *Can you lovingly embrace the person you are right now?*
>
> *Can you wholeheartedly respect the person you are right now?*
>
> *Can you wholeheartedly believe in the person you are right now?*
>
> *Can you wholeheartedly treat your present self with kindness and love?*
>
> *Do you feel that your personality is wonderful just as it is?*
>
> *Do you believe that you have outstanding talents?*
>
> *Right now, are you a radiantly shining being?*
>
> *Are you able to maintain a positive way of living?*

If your answer to these questions is *no*, it is evidence that your perception of yourself is mistaken. You are under the illusion that what is not your original, true self is indeed the real you.

My adoptive father, Masahisa Goi,[2] explains it this way:

The essential nature of a human being is not karmic or sinful. A human being is a life branching out from the one great universal divine source. Each human being is always

guided and protected by the love and wisdom of his or her
guardian spirits and divinities.[3] *All the sufferings of this*
world occur when human beings' mistaken thoughts, from
past existences up to the present, emerge and take shape at
the time of vanishing away.[4]

My own experience confirms the truth of these words. Originally, a human being is a divine life, and not inherently sinful. This is what we originally are. The self that is tarnished and sinful is not the true you or the true me. It is a manifestation of the mistaken thoughts we have held from past lifetimes up to and including the present one—thoughts which are in the process of *fading away* (see Appendix I). When we cling to this past self that is fading away and believe it to be our real self, that is an illusion. No matter how furiously we are raging with resentment or anger, how forcefully we are swept away by violent emotions, or how deceptively we are behaving toward ourselves or others, these thoughts and actions do not represent our true being.

If we look at these aspects of our self and mistakenly believe that our true self is far removed from the divine mind, and that we are a tarnished and sinful existence that cannot possibly be salvaged, then for as long as we live, we will never make happiness our own. It is utterly mistaken to go on blaming and judging ourselves, cheating and lying to ourselves, belittling ourselves, and persecuting ourselves. The discordant self that we are looking at is not who we truly are. It is but a shadow cast by the dark, negative thoughts that cover up this entire world. We have attuned our own mental waves to these waves of dark thoughts. Why should there be any need for our present self to do this? Our mind is already united with the infinite, eternally shining divine vibration of life itself. We are residing in the divine mind, which is perfectly unsullied and undamaged. What is it that still makes us feel frightened and threatened? How come we still feel lost and unfulfilled?

Uncovering a new *you*

Up to now, your life may have been based in misunderstanding and illusion. But you are no longer living that way. The *you* who exists at this moment is totally different from the former you, because you are no longer living in a world of misunderstanding and illusion. The *you* who is reading these words is the true *you*. You are a radiantly shining divine being who has risen above the world of misunderstanding and illusion, and who conveys a true way of living to people who are not yet aware of it. You are not criticized or blamed by anyone. You are not held back or dragged down by anyone. On the contrary, you are respected, admired, and praised by everyone. Today, you are beginning to walk along a radiant, truth-filled, divine path.

If you still do not feel confident in yourself, I suggest you turn your attention to all the bright attributes that are already inscribed in your genes, and draw them out, one by one, into this world where you reside. I am absolutely certain that you can do this. If there is something you wish for or aspire to, tell yourself that it already exists inside you. Call on and draw forth the infinite wisdom and ability that dwell within you, until your heartfelt wish takes shape in this world. Do not be swayed by the dark, negative thoughts that assail you from all around. Instead, decisively draw forth the radiant power and energy that reside within you.

You are essentially a perfect, divine being. You possess all manner of talents and abilities. Is there any need for you to hesitate or waver? You might hesitate to draw forth what belongs to someone else, but when it comes to waking up and drawing out your own inner resources, why should you hold back?

Everyone, please take a good look inside yourselves and open the secret door within your heart—the tightly shut door to your inner self that is filled with infinite potential, infinite ability, infinite energy, and infinite talent. Once that door is open, eternal happiness, eternal youth, health, and eternal life will be restored within you. Thus, by your own hands, you will draw out your infinite happiness and exhibit it to the world.

Originally published in Japanese, December 1990

The Sacred Terrain
of the Divine Mind

The workings of cause and effect

*I*t is true that, for as long as we live with an earth-
bound consciousness, the course of our life pro-
ceeds according to the set law known as the law of cause
and effect. What it means is that, if we constantly let
thoughts of discontent, anger, jealousy, anxiety, fear, pain,
and sadness dominate our mind, sooner or later those
very same kinds of conditions will have to take shape in
our life.

That is to say, each of us is now creating the conditions that will appear in our future. Our daily life is a
series of choices and decisions, made from moment to

moment. By 'choices and decisions,' I mean the thoughts and emotions that we entertain in our consciousness from one moment to the next.

For a great many of us, I think, the flow of our thoughts goes like this: *He is driving me mad! He makes me so angry, I wish he would simply die and disappear from my life!* Then, the next moment, a different feeling arises: *If only he would change his attitude I could forgive and forget... After all, I made some mistakes too...* Then again, *No! I will never forgive him! I have been patient with him, but he doesn't even notice it. He blames me for everything, and thinks he has done nothing wrong. He sees only my weaknesses, never my strong points. He treats me like a fool!*

In ways like this, all sorts of thoughts and emotions race round in our heads, appearing and disappearing from moment to moment. In this state, we ourselves may not even know how we truly feel. When our mind sways back and forth like this, we are unable to discern what is true and real. We just ride on the waves of our surging emotions, sometimes reverting to violent thoughts like: *I wish he would die and leave this earth!* In choosing this kind of thought again and again, we are sending out a stream of intensely negative vibrations to the other person.

In the end, who has to take responsibility for those negative vibrations? Undeniably, it is the person who emitted them—we ourselves. It is a law of this world that whatever we send out, be it positive or negative, will inevitably return to us. *I wish he would die! I wish he would disappear!* If we keep thinking thoughts like these, we can be sure that, sooner or later, the same kinds of thoughts will be sent back to us from someone, somewhere. This is what I mean when I say that each of us must accept the consequences of our own choices and decisions, and take responsibility for them.

Opening a space in our mind

Once we have been caught in the spinning whirlpools of emotionally charged thinking, it takes considerable attention to free ourselves from them. As a first step, it will be helpful if we can train ourselves not to express those emotions in words.

What should we do if we feel overcome with anger and agitation, and are about to express our feelings with hurtful, negative words? If we are aware of our innate divine nature and the creative power of consciousness, and are able to pause and take a deep breath, this can help us to calm our thoughts and soften our words. As a result, a totally different future can unfold for us.

When we stop for a moment and take a deep breath, a space opens up in our mind where we can take another look at ourselves and make a different choice. That one brief moment is a crossroads from which we can guide our life in either a brighter or a darker direction.

After that, our next step is to consider the thoughts that we hold in our mind. Our day-to-day thoughts constantly reveal themselves in our character and personality. Not only that, the path we are walking along now, in this lifetime, was created with our own past consciousness. When our day-to-day consciousness is concerned only with our own needs and wishes, and with arranging things for our own convenience, we make choices that are not aligned with our original being—our innate divine consciousness. These choices then invite negative consequences that are also unaligned with our divine truth.

On the other hand, when we have a clear understanding of our intrinsic nature, we already know, before making choices, what is important and what we should consider. Because of this, we open our eyes to a way of living that is less about our own benefit and more about the benefit of others. Therefore, we never base our choices on our own personal wishes alone. Because the choices we make from moment to moment are mainly for the well-being of others, we are always in tune with our divine consciousness.

When we make choices with this kind of high-dimensional consciousness, all our choices are based in love, light, and truth. They arise directly from our wish for the peace and happiness of humanity, and thus, they are in perfect oneness with the universal divine mind. As a result, we create for ourselves a peaceful life, filled with gratitude and bliss. We almost never make mistaken decisions, and if we do, we are soon able to rectify them and return to the harmonious way of living that is inscribed in our soul. Because of this, we are never visited by misfortune, sorrow, difficulty, or despair, and a life unfolds for us in which nothing is lacking and everything is perfectly arranged. This is our fundamental, natural way of living.

Accumulating daily efforts

As I have often mentioned, everything comes down to our daily thought-habits. What matters most is what we think and do from day to day. This is because our daily thought-habits construct our life. Those who have grasped this principle are steadily overturning their old, discordant thought-habits and transforming them into light. I call these people 'divine-minded people.'

Everything in our life arises from what is in our heart and mind. If there are no negative thoughts or feelings inside us, then nothing negative can take shape in our life. The thoughts and actions of divine-minded people are like beautiful, precious flowers that shine with joy, gratitude, peace, and bliss, and spread pure and noble seeds for future generations. Therefore, it is my cherished hope that even one more person in this world will make divine connections that will brighten their own future as well as the future of earth.

What I mean by 'divine connections' is that, when we live in tune with our inner, divine self, we naturally come in contact with other people who do the same. Through these connections, we encourage and inspire one another, sharing joy, blessings, and peace. Ultimately, this is how all people are meant to live. For, by nature, every human being is a divine-minded person. Deep down, every human being imagines and wishes to believe that all of us are essentially good—that all of us are honest, genuine, truthful, and pure-minded. At present, however, we seldom see this wish manifesting itself in the world around us (think: *infinite betterment!*[5]).

Most of us, even if we have a good heart, are not manifesting our intrinsic divine nature. While we live in a materialistic society, our thoughts and actions tend to be a mixture of good and bad. We get angry, we feel sad, and we criticize others. At times we are kind, helpful, and caring, and at other times we refuse to admit our errors or apologize for them. We tell lies and make excuses, and try to get through life as comfortably as possible while making as little effort as we can.

Even those whom we can now describe as 'divine-minded' were not always noble, deeply loving beings, filled with wisdom and intuition. In the past, most were just average people with good hearts who lived according to the preconceived notions of society as a whole. Most were not creating radiant lives for themselves. Even if they knew about divine principles, they needed more effort and self-belief in order to dismiss all kinds of doubts and confusion from their minds and turn all their thoughts toward the positive. They needed to record bright words in their minds at all times, from moment to moment and day to day.

Entering the terrain of the divine mind is never a

direct gift from God or a favor received from someone else. Ultimately, in order to deeply comprehend our inner divine truth, we must diligently and patiently learn each lesson, one by one. A divine-minded person knows that just learning more and more truths with our intellect is not sufficient. We have to make truth our own, manifesting it in our thoughts and actions. We must crystallize our divine truth and inscribe it in our soul, again and again. We must build up a stockpile of bright, positive words and store them within us. We must keep issuing powerful commands to ourselves with words such as *Love others! Bring out the 'you' who is filled with wisdom and intuition! Call forth your limitless potential and ability! Send out infinite divine light, power, and energy to the world! Be the pure-minded 'you,' the honest and forthright 'you,' so that when others see you, they will be able to naturally sense the presence of divinity!*

Our emergence as a divine-minded person is never a coincidence. Rather, it results from the dedicated efforts we have made again and again, unbeknown to anyone. Among these efforts, the first thing we need to do is overcome our tendency to be ruled by our long-standing assumptions and fixed ideas. This requires an unshakable sense of purpose and self-belief. At times, we may harbor doubts and illusions, and at times we may feel tempted to give up, but we can rise above these distractions as we continue to put truth into practice step by step. There are a good number of people on earth who have already done so.

On the other hand, if we simply ride along on the currents of society's fixed ideas and expectations, we will never be able to draw out our divine truth. Even after death, it will not become clear to us. Until we make a change in our aims and habits, we will keep repeating the same mistakes again and again, in one lifetime after another.

The common assumptions and moral codes of our society are not a sufficient means for eliminating strife from this world and enabling people to live in peace. Rather, they promote a materialistic way of living in a materialistic world. In other words, society's assumptions, knowledge, and moral systems cannot guide people to the sacred terrain of the divine mind. They belong to the legacy that we ourselves created through the law of cause and effect.

Under this law, when we carry out dishonorable actions such as robbery, murder, and so on, our lives are beset with despair, difficulty, tragedy, loneliness, and misfortune, and we remain forever trapped within these cycles. On the other hand, when we grasp hold of the principle of *effect and cause*, we can sever the cycles of misery and self-hate and leap into a new way of life filled with happiness, bliss, and love.

Directing our day-to-day thoughts toward the future

Here, I would like to explain the principle of *effect and cause* from the perspective of the law of cause and effect. The principle of *effect and cause* is a way of living that originates from radiant, shining thoughts, free from the shackles of causes that we generated in the past and free from our present negative thought-habits.

It is widely known that under the law of cause and effect, our lives are created and constructed in the 'thought factory' called the mind. For example, if we entertain negative, misguided thoughts, we build up a negative future in our thought factory. How is it that we so readily create thoughts of anxiety, fear, hatred, and discrimination? It is due to the negative thought-habits that we have built up and held on to for a long period of time. If left as they are, our thoughts continue to pour energy into these negative images, giving them more and more power. There is no end to the amount of negativity that we can generate.

We ourselves are the only ones who can put a stop to these negative thoughts. No one else can take the reins of our mind—no one has that right. Only we have control over our own mind.

Until we conquer our negative thoughts and erase the negative images they create, those exact same images are destined to take shape in our life. No matter how much we might lament our situation, no matter how much we might resent and despise others, it will never resolve the matter. No one else is ever to blame. The responsibility lies solely with us.

To avoid getting caught up in cycles of negativity, we must always be heedful of universal divine truth. Indeed, it is because we are turning away from truth that we experience feelings of pain, misfortune, and sorrow. But thanks to these experiences, we are reminded to take another look at ourselves and then discern the reality.

We need to know that all the conditions in our life are constructed through the cyclical movement of causes and effects. For this reason, it is vital that we have an awareness of our essential divine nature, bringing it into our consciousness step by step. For as long as we remain mindlessly unaware, we will never escape from unhappy circumstances.

If we look at unhappy people the world over, we inevitably find their consciousness to be dark and negative. They are not living vibrantly and radiantly, making the most of life. They are constantly fretting with anxiety, worry, and fear, and have difficulty feeling confident in themselves. They find it easier to imitate others, making the same choices and decisions as others do, and they are unable to take charge of creating their own lives.

No matter who we are, our life in the material world is bound to contain some misfortune and pain. At these times, when a negative incident or circumstance is manifesting in order to fade away and disappear, many of us tend to seize hold of our negative thoughts and feelings, clutching them tightly and refusing to let them go. In doing so, we further reinforce our feelings of sadness and fear. Because we keep holding on to past causes, not knowing how to let go of these conditions that appeared in order to fade away and vanish forever, we keep sending more of the same negative energy into our future, with thoughts such as: *Life is painful, I want to die, It's impossible*, and *It's too much for me*. In this way, we end up caught in a vicious cycle, allowing the thoughts we generate in this moment to create more difficulty and pain in our future.

But with the principle of *effect and cause*, we send our thought-energy in a completely different direction. Suppose we have been generating a series of negative thoughts. By the law of cause and effect, we will have to receive the consequences of those thoughts. Yet, even if we are suddenly thrust into the depths of misfortune, by activating the principle of *effect and cause*, we have the power to vastly change our future through the choices and decisions we make at that time.

In that case, the thing to do is not to get caught up in our circumstances, lamenting and grieving over our misfortune. We do not want to pour any more energy into this negative situation. Instead, we can think: *What is taking place now has manifested as a consequence of some cause generated in the past, and I need to accept it. Through this process, the cause will fade away and disappear, so from this moment on, I will direct my thoughts toward the future.* Then, we can fill our mind with radiant images of our future. When we do, we will be able to firmly believe: *I will keep sending out positive thoughts in order to build a bright and happy future. I will let go of negative thoughts. At present, I am facing difficult circumstances, but this misfortune cannot go on forever. I will not let it go on!*

Now that I have accepted the consequences of my past

negative words and actions, they are behind me. The past is behind me, and a new, radiant life begins today. If we can decisively turn our thoughts toward the light in this way, then a bright and happy future will indeed manifest in our life. This is the principle of *effect and cause*.

So that all of us can enjoy this kind of radiant life, it is essential that every human being, without a single exception, learns and understands their essential divine nature. In so doing, everyone will naturally adopt a positive way of living. The birth of even one more divine-minded person is a great leap forward toward peace on earth and the happiness of humanity. For as long as there are divine-minded people in this world, the planet will surely be able to advance.

Originally published in Japanese, April 2012

The Indispensable Role
of Divine-Minded People

Why can't we acknowledge our divinity?

*A*s human beings, each one of us is meant to be seeking out and pursuing our inner divine self. And yet, when it comes to this quest, many of us feel lost and hesitate to move forward.

What is it that makes us so timid with regard to our inner divinity? What on earth is it that frightens us away from acknowledging our own divine nature? Our inner self is pure goodness, filled with light and love. Yet we are afraid to acknowledge ourselves as divine beings, as if we were innately flawed. This way of thinking is an illusion—the manifestation of causes carried over from previous lifetimes, compounded with our various habitual thought patterns, our lack of self-confidence, and our excessive concern about what others think.

In other words, most of us are living out our lives unaware of our starting point—our primary purpose—which is to construct and create our lives with our own God-given power. We have not fully grasped what it means to be alive. We are convinced that we are not capable of living on our own, and that someone else must teach us and guide us. We feel that we can get through life only by imitating what others do.

The mirror of our consciousness

I think that many of us may be in the habit of looking in the mirror each morning as we start our day. When we look in the mirror, the mirror faithfully reflects our face, our expression, and our physical form, just as they are.

If we look tired and worn out, or if we are lacking in confidence, the mirror will show it. If we are out of sorts, the mirror will reflect our anxious gaze, our washed-out complexion, and our severe expression. It shows whether our heart is radiant or not, whether we are full of energy or not, whether we have a strong sense of purpose, whether we are filled with love, and whether we are in a state of harmony. All of this is reflected in our physical countenance.

Our consciousness is also a kind of mirror. It is a mirror through which we can see two worlds—an inner world and an outer world. The inner world depicts our original, essential self. This is our divine self—our noble, radiant, loving self that is truth itself and the universe itself. The outer world depicts our physically-minded self—our daily thoughts, our shifting emotions, and the various events and phenomena that take shape around us.

These two depictions of our self—our inner, divine self and our outer, physically-minded self where thoughts and emotions appear and disappear—will eventually join together as one. This is our purpose in living. However, when the mirror of our consciousness becomes smudged or clouded over, the inner world—our true, divine self— is no longer portrayed. All that is reflected is our outer, physical self, the self that keeps shifting and wavering in response to the changing conditions that manifest in our life.

In the far distant past, human beings could freely come and go between the inner and outer worlds. But as time passed, the mirror of our consciousness became clouded over. Dust collected on it, followed by dirt and grime, until it could no longer fulfill its original purpose. It became unable to depict our inner divine image. And accordingly, we human beings forgot the mirror's original purpose.

When the mirror of our consciousness could no longer reflect our essential, divine image, all that we could see were our superficial attributes. The mirror ceased to portray the world of the heart and mind—the true world, the world of God.

Polishing the mirror of our consciousness

Despite this, the inner world still exists as firmly as ever, and our mind still has its innate ability to freely move to and from that inner world. But in order to do this, we have to polish the mirror of our consciousness, which has become cloudy and tarnished by selfish greed, emotional fixations, and habitual ways of thinking. Once we have wiped away all these smudges, the mirror will reflect our true self once again.

How do we polish the mirror of our consciousness? To do this, we need to have a cleaning cloth. Thankfully, a cleaning cloth has already been given to us. This cleaning cloth is our own physical being—our physical body along with our surface thoughts and emotions. When ailments or sufferings appear in our physical body, it means that our body is serving as a cleaning cloth, removing smudges that have built up on the mirror of our consciousness. The same can be said about the various shifting thoughts that pass through our physical brain. When they appear, it means that the grime and smudges that have built up on the mirror of our consciousness are now being wiped away on the cleaning cloth of our physical being.

Because it is always working hard to clean the mirror of our consciousness, this cleaning cloth can get very dirty, and so it needs to be washed. The way we wash it is through practices like light-filled thinking and prayer for world peace (please see the appendices for more on these and other practices). When we pray for world peace, we connect with a tremendously powerful, purifying divine light that works like a cleaning agent. The dirt that covers our cleaning cloth is marvelously washed away. And at the same time, this divine cleaning agent spreads out widely and washes the cleaning cloths of all humanity.

As we diligently continue to pray for world peace, little by little the smudged mirror of our consciousness will be cleaned and polished, and in the polished spaces that emerge, our true, radiant image will be reflected. Parts of our true, divine self—our bright, positive, courageous, loving, thankful, and forgiving self—will begin to shine through as we steadily polish the mirror of our consciousness. Through this process, the true purpose of our life becomes clear, and our desire to elevate and polish ourselves grows stronger. Before long, we find ourselves overflowing with hope and joy.

As the mirror of our consciousness becomes increasingly polished and our way of living becomes more and more filled with light, finally the day will come when the entire mirror sparkles like new. From within the mirror, all at once, our true self—our radiant, divine self—will appear. This self will meet our outer physical self, and they will merge perfectly into one. This is how we can live as divine beings in the physical, earthly world.

Purifying the world of negative thoughts

At present, there are a precious number of people who are earnestly striving to live each day in accordance with their innate divine nature. Although their inner and outer worlds have not yet merged into one, they are no longer standing outside the mirror of consciousness. Rather, they have passed through the mirror and come in contact with their inner self. These are the ones whom I call 'divine-minded people.'

If we give no consideration to our divine nature and adamantly refuse to accept it, then the mirror of our consciousness will continue to grow cloudier and more tarnished, and our inner world will remain completely closed off to us. In this state, we are a long way from being lifted out of our misery and misfortune. The reason why is that no one is going to polish our mirror for us. No matter how much power and authority, how much fame and honor, how much money, how high an education, or how many people we might have supporting and assisting us, no one is going to step in and polish our mirror for us. Unless we take it upon ourselves to polish and elevate our being, the mirror of our consciousness cannot possibly depict our true image.

Because the world around us is filled with chaos and confusion, negativity, contradictions, and illusions, it is very difficult for us human beings to turn our minds to the inner world. Unlike the inner world, the outer world is overrun with the turbulent energy of negative thoughts. Because of this, every second of every minute of every hour, someone—or rather, a great many people—fall victim to this turbulent energy and are absorbed into its flow. Humanity's collective thought-energy is bringing about this phenomenon.

Every day, each and every one of us is generating and sending out negative thoughts—thoughts of discontent, anger, resentment, vengeance, sorrow, distress, fear, anxiety, conflict, and so on. No one takes responsibility for these negative thoughts. Everyone flings around whatever thoughts and emotions they like, sending them out across the world.

The force of all these negative emotional thoughts creates an incredibly powerful vortex of turbulent energy. Unable to fade away and disappear, those masses of thought-energy settle into places where disharmony has occurred, and they hang about in that space. Those who happen to be in that place, or who are passing by, can fall victim to this unseen turbulent energy. Under the influence of its violent waves, they may end up getting involved in an accident, becoming suddenly irritated, or upset, or being assailed by fear and anxiety.

Meanwhile, there are also people in this world who are extinguishing and purifying all this unseen negative thought-energy. These are the divine-minded people who are praying day in and day out for peace on earth, and steadily sending out waves of gratitude, light, love, and large-scale harmony. Such people are indispensable for humanity's evolution and spiritual awakening.

The special right of divine-minded people

Once we have begun to elevate our own thoughts and connect with our inner divine nature, we are on the road to becoming a divine-minded person. As we continue along this road, we are bringing glimmers of light to people who are living amidst the interminable waves of misfortune (think: *infinite light!*) that run rampant on this earth.

Even now, the mere existence of divine-minded people in this world and their continuous prayers for world peace are gradually healing and lessening the world's misfortune and sorrow. Eventually, all unhappy, tragic phenomena will cease, and all harmful, negative activities will come to a standstill. This transformation will begin around each divine-minded person and spread outward.

Any tragedy or misfortune that lies in the path of a divine-minded person has no power to sway that person.

Even if they should meet with a terrible accident or disaster, they never allow it to penetrate their soul—their inner divine being. This is because their soul is light itself, and does not attract any negative vibrations.

When we are involved in an accident or calamity, when we are assailed by an illness, when the threat of vengeance or betrayal makes us fear for our life, or when we are lamenting our adverse fortune, we become painfully aware of the power of our fate. We can easily feel completely at a loss and thrown into a daze. However, the noble, sacred soul within us—our inner divine self—does not attract or call forth any of those negative conditions, nor does it permit them to find their way in. This is the special right afforded to divine-minded people.

Only what we desire can appear

Divine-minded people know that in this lifetime, everything that takes place—everything that happens to us—is given shape and brought about by our own thoughts, words, and actions, from either the recent or the ancient past. All the fruits that we reap are the results of seeds that we ourselves have been sowing day in and day out. The universal law, or universal truth, stipulates that not a single thing can come to pass which our deep, inner mind was not willing to accept.

Even when something unanticipated pops up suddenly in our life, that too is an outcome of the thoughts, words, and actions that we have continuously sent out over a long period of time. With our family, at work, at school, in the hospital—wherever we might go and whatever we are doing—every person we encounter, and every single incident and phenomena that takes place throughout our life is the result of our own daily thoughts, words, and actions—nothing else. Indeed, not a single thing happens that we ourselves have not in some way wished for.

So, the question is, what are we wishing for? Naturally, we are free to choose what we wish for. It is entirely up to our own free will.

The only things that occur in our life are the things that we ourselves have willed, and it is up to each of us to decide what we wish for. All the events and circumstances that take shape in our life, whether good or bad, are the products of our own thoughts, words, and actions. They can guide us to happiness or send us plunging into misery.

It may be that, at present, disagreeable conditions and circumstances are taking shape in our life. But once we begin to seek out our true, divine self and steadily pray for world peace, there is no doubt that, in time, we will absolutely be able to overturn those negative phenomena. Prayer for world peace, in and of itself, is a powerful method for awakening to our true self, and for shattering and transforming the negative, habitual view of ourselves that we have held up to now. As our inner divine nature is revived in our soul, we will find ourselves enjoying a happy life filled with love, forgiveness, and wisdom.

Evasion or acceptance

As human beings, all of us are affected by the incidents and events that come to pass in this phenomenal world. How do we respond to these phenomena once they have occurred? Do we run away from them, or do we accept and embrace them?

If we run away, our fate never improves. We remain at the same stage in our evolution, or we might even fall back. On the other hand, if we accept the events and circumstances that come our way, we draw forth a marvelous power to overturn the situation, and we find ourselves greeting a marvelous turning point in our life.

If we had run away, the same situation or circumstance would have been created all over again, but when we accept the situation as it is, immediately, our inner divine light shines forth, and in that moment, the conditions that would have repeated themselves are extinguished before they can manifest.

How do we find the courage and determination to accept and embrace any incident or phenomenon that takes shape in our life? The best method I know of is my mentor Masahisa Goi's teaching of *Fading away—May peace prevail on Earth.* Goi Sensei, as he was known, explained that all the unwelcome phenomena that appear in our life are brought about by causes generated in the past—mainly in our previous lifetimes—and that they are appearing now in order to fade away and vanish forever. Thus, he said, the thing to do is to accept those incidents and circumstances without fear or hesitation, regarding them as phenomena that are in the process of fading away, and fling them into our prayers for world peace. (For more on this practice, please see Appendices I and II.)

Those who are already aware of their inner divine nature, although they might momentarily feel unsettled or upset, are able to immediately think, *It will definitely get better! It's absolutely all right!* They can accept any incident that they encounter, and, in accordance with their thoughts, a future opens up for them in which things are, indeed, absolutely all right.

The various phenomena and incidents that take shape are, in themselves, nothing more than the effects of thoughts, words, and actions that we generated in the past, being delivered to us now in accordance with the law of cause and effect. They are simply manifestations. Depending on whether or not our soul accepts these phenomena, our life will turn in either a better or worse direction. If we are able to face up to the stream of events that occur in our life and, one by one, transform them into light through our prayers for peace, we will have not a single thing to worry about or fear.

The power of our belief

We earthly human beings have long been convinced that our suffering and sorrow are imposed on us by people and events that we encounter in our life. But actually, it is just the reverse. We ourselves draw those people and events toward us, and what they do to us is the bidding of our own will. The more we lie to others, judge and blame others, and burn with hatred and vengeance, the more lies and deceptions will come our way, and the more judgment, blame, hatred, and vengeance will surround us, triggering negative events and circumstances to take shape.

In contrast, those who regularly engage in practices like prayer for world peace (see appendices) are, with their own will, attracting the benefits of those positive words and actions into their lives.

When we dedicate ourselves in service to others, to humanity, and to the entire world in this way, we will undoubtedly see our thoughts, wishes, and desires accomplished. This is because practices like prayer for world peace are in tune with the laws of the universe, and through them, we draw forth circumstances and phenomena that also accord with the laws of the universe—circumstances of infinite happiness, prosperity, success, joy, health, and so on.

Whether we doubt this reality or believe in it is completely up to us. If we continually harbor doubts, we will attract more doubt and suspicion. If we believe firmly, we will draw forth trust and belief. Doubt and disbelief create a life of indecision, difficulty, pain, setbacks, uneasiness, anxiety, and fear, while belief and trust create a life in which there is no uncertainty or muddiness—a radiant life of peace, tranquility, and joy.

As we acquire a stronger sense of belief, little by little we are freed from our doubt and uncertainty. All human beings yearn, at least a little, to attain a state of unshakeable belief. As we acquire this kind of firm belief, we become able to embrace the unexpected, unfortunate events that come up in our life and transform them into experiences of growth and self-creation.

When we have fully made this power of belief our own, the circumstances and phenomena that appear before us will no longer be our enemy. No matter what might happen, we will transform it into an object of forgiveness, gratitude, and joy in our soul. By means of our inner spiritual light, we will heal our troubled, doubt-filled heart and dissolve our anxiety and fear. What is more, we will be completely free of the past in which we confronted countless obstacles, setbacks, and misfortunes.

The very act of believing goes far beyond our imagination, bringing about a wondrous display of divine power. Not only does this power protect us from harm, it also has a positive effect on the people around us.

The present state of this world is that waves of doubt and uncertainty are constantly waiting to jump in and take control of our mind. When allowed to run free, doubt takes on a power of its own and grows stronger. If it escalates to a certain point, no amount of knowledge or intelligence can put the brakes on it. This is how our feelings of doubt become the spark that ignites disputes, conflicts, and wars.

What is most essential, therefore, is for each and every one of us to resolve our doubtful mindset and believe in our innate divine nature. This is first and foremost. We need to be fully aware that when we give free rein to doubt, it will attract all kinds of negative circumstances into our lives.

Doubtful, negative thoughts can only thrive amidst a low-dimensional vibration. But when we pray whole-heartedly for world peace, our dimensional level rises. As this happens, the light we emit grows brighter, illuminating humanity's dark thoughts until they vanish away in the light. The low-dimensional vibration transforms and is absorbed into a high-dimensional one. In this way, as we raise the earth's vibration to a higher dimensional level, dark, negative thoughts will naturally die out of their own accord.

We are the universe

This is sure to happen because in truth, the universe is originally perfect, and each and every one of us is made up of the very same structure as the great universe. Each of us has the same structure as the whole, or God itself.

Or rather, we can say that this structure is replicated in each human being. In every part of us, no matter how small, the same framework that makes up the whole is replicated. In our brain, in our blood, in each one of our cells, in our genes, and in our heart and mind flows the same system that exists throughout the universe. Even if we were to take the smallest, most minor part of ourselves and break it up into sub-microscopic, infinitesimally small pieces, we would find that within each one of those pieces, the universal fabric—the framework of God—is replicated. We could also say that it is passed down.

This incredible feat takes place across the entire universe. What this means is that the grace of God pervades our brain, our blood, each one of our cells, our genes, and our heart and mind. God's infinite creativity, infinite wisdom, and infinite evolution are woven right into our being. When we take time to study and investigate this truth, we cannot help but marvel at the structure and workings of the universe.

Accordingly, all living things on this earth are governed by the universal law. The universal law is in the pulse and the DNA of every single human being. This law guides the oceans, the rivers, the clouds, and the rain, and all the stars and galaxies in the night sky. The origin and evolution of all life are also based on this law.

Even if our ways of thinking, our values, and our creative impulses appear different, each and every one of our lives is rooted in this intrinsic law. What is this law? It is none other than the universal divine mind. Although everything in the universe seems a separate and distinct entity, in truth, everything is firmly interconnected by threads of the invisible and unfathomable universal divine light, and everything is living in accordance with the universal law.

When we look at it this way, we can see that divine life is continuously pulsating within our blood, within our genes, and within our thoughts. Those who can readily believe this are people who are especially cherished and needed by the universal God. They possess a singular value in this world.

Each and every day, let us live radiantly and vibrantly! Let us go on living with infinite potential and infinite hope, until the day when we wake up in the morning and find that we have merged into one with the divine being that resides in the mirror of our consciousness.

Originally published in Japanese, July 2001

Creating Bright Conditions in Our Lives

The shared aim of science and religion

What is God? Since long, long ago, human beings have believed in a divine creative force, and have eagerly tried to demonstrate its existence. Why does humanity have such a yearning for and fascination with God? The reason, I think, is that God is the essence of human life.

All human beings possess a consciousness. All of us possess a heart and mind, emotions and thoughts. And yet, hardly anyone reflects upon what it means to have a heart, mind, and consciousness. Almost no one is aware that consciousness comes from God, and that

God resides within our own life.

Up to now, we human beings have sought what is unknown and mysterious mainly by researching the world around us. Very few of us have tried to discover those mysteries within ourselves. In both religion and science, we have reached further and further outward in our quests. Yet if we take this inquiry to a deeper level, we must eventually plunge into our inner self.

In the vast treasure house that exists within us, the pursuits of science and the quests of religion come together and become one and the same. This is because in the ultimate sense, both science and religion share the same aim. Each of them is a means for uncovering the limitless potential of a human being, and of showing us that from the very beginning, every human being has been provided with a perfect array of unlimited aptitudes and capabilities.

Doubting and believing

At all times, science places a high priority on proof. We may theorize that infinite potential and infinite ability reside within all humanity, but so far, science cannot support this premise with actual proof. To verify this claim, scientists would have to spend their entire lives working to prove it.

The world of religion and spirituality, on the other hand, is a world founded on belief and intuitive knowledge. Unlike the path of science, religion does not start off by doubting and questioning things.

We human beings are free to choose whichever path we prefer. It is up to each of us to choose the approach we like best—science or religion, doubt or belief.

Which is an easier path for us to follow—doubt or belief? Overwhelmingly, humanity has preferred the path of doubt. The majority of people find it very difficult to believe in something unquestioningly. And indeed, doubt and uncertainty have given impetus to humanity's progress and development. Through the path of science, we aim for a true understanding of our existence by seeking answers to our uncertainties.

Doubting begins with rejecting and denying things, while believing means actively accepting them. However, the kind of belief that I am thinking of here is not a blind belief that comes from ignorance. Rather, it is a path that is illuminated by deep intuition and wisdom.

Although humanity's doubt has led us to make many noteworthy innovations, it has also brought about untold misery and suffering. All of the conflicts, wars, famines, and other tragedies of the 20th century were born from doubt and distrust. We distrusted other peoples and ethnic groups, we distrusted their religious beliefs, and we doubted in their abilities. We even looked at ourselves with mistrustful eyes, doubting in our own talents, abilities, attributes, disposition, character, and background.

There is nothing so harsh and pitiable as being unable to trust and believe in ourselves. When we distrust ourselves, we end up rejecting ourselves and denying our own worth. Our self-doubt influences the people around us, undermining their own confidence as well. It spreads first to our parents and children, then to the rest of our family, our friends, acquaintances, and further on to our community and our nation. As doubt continues to escalate, it finally erupts in the form of disputes, violent conflicts, and wars.

In contrast, there is nothing so wonderful as trust and belief. This is because deep within our being, beyond such surface emotions as doubt and distrust, lie the origins of peace, harmony, quietude, serenity, and love. It is from these origins that happiness and gratitude flow forth.

The only way we can trust and accept others is to first

trust and believe in ourselves. Being able to believe in ourselves is the ultimate joy in life.

To my way of thinking, the significance of both science and spiritual pursuits lies in the extent to which they enable us to draw forth our inner divinity—our infinite capabilities—without needing to rely on others, cling to others, or make entreaties to others. My aim is to strike a balance between science and spirituality, so that all people can guide themselves to their own ultimate state of happiness and bliss.

Talking of unhappiness reinforces unhappiness

Each one of us unconditionally has the potential to attain true happiness. What has happened, however, is that our self-doubts have created an ongoing stream of difficulties and misfortunes in our lives. As a result, we have all but forgotten what true happiness feels like. Instead, we take a grim satisfaction in moaning about our troubles, talking about them to others and eliciting other people's sympathy.

But in so doing, we cause our misfortunate circumstances to become more deeply entrenched. Repeating the same cheerless words again and again to ourselves and to others only serves to reinforce our unhappiness. On top of that, by continuing to give others a strong impression of unhappiness, we are intentionally making it harder and harder for ourselves to exit from our misfortunate circumstances. This is a textbook example of rejecting and denying the preciousness of life.

No matter how bitter, destitute, and painful our circumstances might be, we must make up our mind to refrain from speaking words that will further intensify our suffering. If we do happen to speak such words, we will still be all right if we quickly abandon them and make efforts to create a brighter situation. To assist us in doing this, I heartily recommend the method of *Fading away—May peace prevail on Earth* that was introduced by my mentor and adoptive father, Masahisa Goi (see Appendix I).

Whatever difficulty we may be experiencing—the pain of illness, the anguish of disharmony and conflict, or the sorrow of losing a loved one—when we cannot bear it alone, we lessen our suffering by talking about it with the people around us. By talking with others, our sorrow and pain can be cut in half, and our joys can be doubled. However, we mustn't forget that if we continue using negative words again and again, we will end up adding to our pain and unhappiness.

Fading away—May peace prevail on Earth

Most of us can't help wanting to talk to someone about our unfortunate situation, our lack of money, or whatever is afflicting us. If we choose to talk about these things it is all right, but then we must act to clear away the negative words we have spoken.

This is where the method of *Fading away—May peace prevail on Earth* plays its role. When we fling our negative words into the midst of this peace prayer, our heart and mind are uplifted, and the person we were speaking to will not retain our negative words in their mind, either. In that moment, with the thought-activity of *Fading away—May peace prevail on Earth*, both we and the other person reside within the vibration of the great divine light that is the prayer for world peace. This vibration, in and of itself, is infinite harmony, infinite happiness, infinite peace, joy, and healing.

The more we go on talking about our pain and unhappiness, the longer those unpleasant circumstances persist, and the more difficult it becomes for us to get out of our situation. This is because we are using negative words over and over again, never tiring of it. The method of *Fading away—May peace prevail on Earth* allows us to

nullify those negative words and halt the cycle of intensi-
fying our negative circumstances.

Once we know about our innate divine nature, this
'fading away' method is easy to accept and put into practice. And after practicing it for some time, we find that we
no longer give voice to negative thoughts and feelings at
all, but quickly dispel them within the great bright light
of our prayerful mind. Even amidst suffering, misfortune,
grief, and pain, we are able to find a little joy and happiness, and that is what we speak about to others. As we
repeat these positive words and feelings, before we know
it our sorrow, grief, and pain begin to fade away, and our
happiness and joy increase, eventually becoming our
reality.

This is only natural. When we stop talking—to others
and to ourselves—about our pain and unhappiness, the
laws of truth dictate that those negative circumstances will not be aggravated any further. On the contrary,
because we are able to find even the slightest modicum
of happiness and joy amidst our suffering—and keep
cultivating those good feelings—they can take root and
grow ever stronger.

Creating bright conditions in our lives

Whatever circumstances we might find ourselves in, if we continue speaking with a view to happiness, health, and abundance, then without a doubt, we will each be able to create those bright conditions in our own life.

This is a way of living based on the principle of *effect and cause*. Even if at present, the law of cause and effect has led us to a thoroughly miserable situation, the principle of *effect and cause* gives us the means to affirm, within those circumstances, the great divine soul that resides in ourselves and in all human beings.

When we speak with a view to the place we are meant to reach—a place of happiness, peace, and belief in our divine nature—then, without fail, we will create the circumstances that we have been talking about. This is a universal law.

Because they are well aware of this, divine-minded people are constantly speaking light-filled words and expressing gratitude to the world of nature (see Appendices III and IV). They have devoted a great deal of energy to developing this habit. Through these positive actions, they are demonstrating to the world a way of living that accords with the harmony of the universe, and are outwardly manifesting their inner radiance.

Without divine-minded people, the 21st century would be just like the 20th, where negative words created tragic conditions like wars, poverty, disease, and famine. This is why I say that the existence of divine-minded people is inexpressibly precious and urgently needed. Each divine-minded person is an immensely great existence, carrying a mission much more important than he or she realizes. Each and every divine-minded person is sowing light-filled seeds all around them. As more and more of these seeds begin to sprout, gradually, humanity's negative thoughts, words, and actions are cleansed and purified.

It is a natural thing for us to talk about ourselves, but we should be aware that the things we say also take shape in other peoples' minds. We need to realize just how influential our words can be. The truth of this becomes clear when we look at the spread of negative words during the 20th century.

When even one more individual starts to live as a divine-minded person, speaking only bright words and affirming the sanctity of all life on earth, we will also see the people around him or her making positive changes in their own ways of living.

100,000 divine-minded people will form a critical mass

During the 21st century, the bright words, prayers, and practices of divine-minded people will create what Dr. Rupert Sheldrake calls a 'morphic field,' or 'a field of morphic resonance.'[6] When the number of divine-minded people reaches the threshold of 100,000, a critical mass will be achieved, and all at once the divine consciousness of humanity will reawaken, so that peace can manifest in this world.

For this to happen, first of all, I feel that more and more people need to understand, accept, and live by the principle of *effect and cause*. I say this because for humanity to find peace through the workings of cause and effect would take an extraordinarily long period of time, and before that could happen the Earth would be destroyed through wars and natural disasters.

Next, each of these divine-minded people will demonstrate the truth that our original, essential state of being is one of health, happiness, and prosperity, and they will convey the ultimate principle that all beings are divine life itself. I believe that when humanity has accepted this principle, wars, conflicts, and strife will cease to exist.

When 100,000 divine-minded people influence others to stop creating illness, illness will soon disappear.

When 100,000 divine-minded people speak only light-filled words, emit only light-filled thoughts, and perform only light-filled actions, each individual's negative thought-habits will change, and soon humanity will no longer experience any negative conditions or events.

When 100,000 divine-minded people demonstrate, by their own hand, their limitless inner capabilities, overturning the endless misfortunes on earth one after another, humanity will no longer rely on people and things outside themselves.

As divine-minded people adopt a way of living based on the principle of *effect and cause*, all human beings will develop a powerful motivation to reach this same state. Even if they cannot achieve it right away, their steadfast desire will guide them there. And from then on, we will enter an era where all issues will be resolved by means of our inner power and abilities.

Through the emergence of 100,000 divine-minded people, it will be made clear that our true, essential human nature is inexpressibly noble, perfect, harmonized, and radiant. The universal divine mind has embedded the truth of our divinity within each and every human being. All human beings are truth itself, divinity itself, and the universe itself. Each and every one of us is a supremely great existence, within which the entire universe dwells. We ourselves are part of that universe, we belong to the universe, and we are structured as creative beings who are able to freely build a radiant way of living.

All we need is a little bit more courage, determination, and belief. We are not the weak, imperfect beings that most of us think ourselves to be. It is only that we have not drawn out our inner self-awareness—the consciousness of *I am able*, and *I am perfect and complete*.

Let us talk of happiness

To encounter the real, true, divine-minded person who exists within us, let us live proactively, in accordance with the principle of *effect and cause*. Rather than dragging up the disappointments and grudges of the past, let us devote all our energy to thinking and speaking of the joyful conditions that we wish to create. When we continually speak words of happiness and gratitude, our words reach the ears of people around us, and little by little, our bright, positive thoughts spread to those people as well. Even if the vast majority of human beings are still speaking of misfortune, war, illness, and poverty, we continue speaking only of harmony, happiness, and health, with a view to our essential divine nature. And through the principle of *effect and cause*, our words and thoughts will take hold in the minds of others.

We should never hesitate to share happiness with others. If no one takes the initiative to talk about happiness, happiness will never come to humanity. For this reason, we need to have as many people as possible talking only about happiness, joy, hope, and other light-filled emotions, without using any negative words at all.

In talking of happiness, we will first of all bring happy circumstances into our own reality. Then, the people around us will begin to align with us and create their own ways of living filled with happiness and gratitude.

There is nothing more gratifying and delightful than seeing the bright, positive words we speak create new circumstances that slowly take root and materialize in our lives. And at the same time, our true, divine nature is naturally becoming manifest. What a great blessing this is! This, in itself, is living by the principle of *effect and cause*.

Originally published in Japanese, May 2001

Reviving the Memory
of Our Divine Self

Resurrecting a dormant truth

*I*n the dimensional space that connects our life with the universe, all living things are linked, by the same unbroken chain, with the great universal life. We human beings also live wholly enveloped within the immense light of this universal life. In every single one of the cells and genes that make up our physical body, infinite truth itself is inscribed. Regardless of where on earth we live, all of us receive the great universal light equally, and all of us are fully enveloped in it.

The great life of the universe transcends space and dimension, extending into infinity. Every living thing, in all corners of the earth and the farthest reaches of the universe, is governed by its laws. The universe is astonishingly grand, full of mysteries, and altogether astounding. We human beings are living—or rather, our life is sustained—within the fathomless divine realm. As such, it seems like our existence as a single human being is but a small, insignificant, worthless existence. This is how many of us see ourselves.

However, nothing could be further from the truth. As human beings, each and every one of us is an individual life branching out from the great life of the universe. That is to say, each one of us is a divine life. Each of us is the offspring of God. Yet, without our noticing it, this ultimate truth has been wiped from our surface awareness. We have become brainwashed, our minds taken over by mistaken ideas and assumptions. The truth of our divine nature, which is inscribed in every single gene that comprises our physical body, has been put to sleep in the depths of our consciousness, where it now lies dormant.

Now, however, at long last we have reached the time when all human beings, without exception, will reawaken to this truth. Already, a significant number of people are accepting the ultimate truth that is inscribed in the genes of their physical body—the mystical truth that exists within all of our genes and has remained eternally unchanged, and the infinite ability and potential that are contained within it. These divine-minded people have started to become aware of the emptiness, the impermanence, and the futility of living without believing in and re-enlivening these innate parts of us. They have realized that they cannot go on living while their essential self continues to slumber.

How can we revive the original power, the amazing potential, and the infinite wisdom that dwell within each and every one of us? It is for this purpose that the world peace prayer has emerged. This prayer method transcends boundaries of religion, ethnicity, background, and ideology, offering us all the opportunity to join together with feelings of mutual respect and understanding. Before long, I believe, practicing this method will lead to a great, positive transformation on a global scale.

Today, the overemphasis on materialism that has dominated our lives for generations is being overturned, thanks to each individual's world peace prayers. The age in which we learned to value superficial attainments such as fame and prestige, status, authority over others, financial power, and academic prowess is coming to an end. Not only do these learned values fail to bring out the infinite capabilities with which we human beings are originally endowed, they can actually suppress these capabilities and paralyze them.

Accumulating mistaken efforts

Many of us believe that we must grab hold of the surface conditions and phenomena that are visible to our eyes, and so we train ourselves to focus our efforts on them at all times. This kind of belief is far removed from our true way of living. For us human beings, to truly 'live' means to express ourselves and conduct ourselves without any falsity. That is all.

Without exception, every single human being is originally furnished with qualities like infinite wisdom and potential. The question is how to draw them out and make the most of them. In this regard, being able to express and conduct ourselves truthfully, genuinely, and unaffectedly, is a precious thing indeed. This is how we naturally guide ourselves to have a healthy body and a radiant life.

It is so important for us human beings to keep ourselves in tune with the laws of nature and the universe, and to bring out the best in ourselves, just as we are. But however good our intentions might be, and no matter how long and hard we study, work, practice, and train ourselves, when we rely solely on our own brain and our own thoughts, we find that, again and again, our endeavors lead us down a mistaken path that is removed from the universal law. Even after many years of blood, tears, perseverance, and fortitude, we can end up guiding ourselves in a mistaken direction. This happens because beliefs that run counter to the universal flow are entrenched in our consciousness, causing damage to our mind and our body. In the 20th century, conventional wisdom led us to repeatedly engage in mistaken efforts and endeavors, and through the ongoing harmful effects of our collective words and actions we have put humankind on a path of destruction and collapse.

This pattern of repeating misguided thoughts and actions over and over, and imprinting them in our brain and body, all due to our fixed ideas and beliefs, is not in our original state of being. We have inscribed in ourselves a set of fixed patterns that are completely unnatural, and it goes without saying that such actions are self-destructive.

Because we have walked for so long on this misguided path, putting ourselves back on our true path is no easy task. It requires time, effort, and diligence dozens of times greater than what it took to train ourselves in mistaken thoughts and actions.

Correcting our mistaken beliefs

The time has arrived when all human beings, without exception, must wake up to the limitless capabilities with which we are originally endowed. The way to draw out these inborn capabilities to the greatest extent possible is through prayer for world peace and a variety of well-chosen self-training practices (please see the appendices for suggestions).

Each of us is free to choose practices that are aligned with the universal law, with a view to fully drawing out our own limitless potential. As we carry out these practices we focus our consciousness on them, with careful attention. As time goes on, we continue to assess the progress that we are making, and adjust our practices to suit our own special qualities and temperament.

When we immerse ourselves in light-filled practices with this kind of single-minded focus, we unknowingly transcend our usual, miscellaneous thoughts, and a radiant world of freedom and harmony—a world of infinite potential—unfolds within us. As we continue to experience this, we increasingly exhibit our infinite abilities, talents, wisdom, and sensibilities. Illnesses, accidents, and disasters are naturally avoided, and everything that happens is perceived in a positive light.

Whatever self-training practices we may choose to engage in, the method of *Fading Away—May peace prevail on Earth* is, I think, of fundamental importance. Through this prayer method, everything in our lives and throughout the world is naturally resolved and brought into harmony, without exertion or strain. Everything is put in perfect order, and everything is guided toward peace and happiness. This is because, through this deep yet simple prayer, the universal law and truth reveal themselves in our life. At the same time, the prayer emits an infinite light and power that corrects the fate of the entire world.

To practice this method, there is no need for anyone to join a religion, or to leave the religion they are presently affiliated with. The words *May peace prevail on Earth* can easily be added at the end of one's own cherished prayers, and the entire phrase—*Fading away—May peace prevail on Earth*—can be used in face of any anxiety, emotion, or circumstance.

Revealing our true self

I have continued teaching the method of *Fading away—
May peace prevail on Earth* (see Appendix I) and offering
related practices in hopes of supporting each individual
in their quest to draw out their own, infinite potential,
while at the same time contributing to the well being of
humanity, the earth, and the world of nature.

Each individual is different, and therefore it is important to ascertain the approach that is best suited to that
person. Offering a hundred, a thousand, or ten thousand
people exactly the same guidance and urging them all to
follow exactly the same path would not only fail to bring
out their innate individual abilities, it could bury those
abilities even deeper inside them. It would be like making
ten thousand people who are all the same, like clones of
one another. They wouldn't gain an understanding of
their true, individual selves. By doing exactly as others
do, they would be unable to believe in their own unique
aptitudes and abilities, and would remain constantly reli-
ant on others, unable to take responsibility for themselves.

Naturally, to create clone-like people who all pursue
happiness in the same way and who all end up unfulfilled would be utterly meaningless. I believe that our

aim should be for each individual to recognize and reveal their own infinite abilities and infinite potential, and, free of worries and doubts, to confidently determine the course of their own future with their own will. This way of living, I feel, is the true path that we human beings are meant to walk along.

I think something similar can be said about animals living in the world of nature. Each species develops different kinds of abilities. Each species, in its own splendid way, ascertains its areas of ability and naturally manifests them to the fullest. For example, a lion, which does not eat fruits, is not manifesting its true potential if it practices climbing trees quickly. Similarly, if a monkey, which does eat fruits, practices running swiftly across the plains like a lion, it will not be able to get the fruits on tall trees. The skills and movements needed for animals to get their food differ widely on the outside, but inside, they are fundamentally the same. Each one is able to survive by cultivating its individual skills and characteristics. So, if a monkey works hard to imitate a lion, or if a lion trains itself to climb trees like a monkey, neither one will learn to exhibit its true nature. The skills and traits that each animal cultivates will differ depending on its objectives.

As for us human beings, no matter how elevated a teaching or how noble a prayer we might have, no matter how perfectly a certain self-training method might be attuned to the universal law, each of us has to understand it and practice it for ourselves. Only then do we bring out the potential to reveal our true, individual self. Even if we were to guide people to deny the infinite abilities that are latent within them and merely imitate others, believing in the products of conventional thinking—it would be like building a house on the sand. If some urgent matter were to arise, their lives would immediately fall apart, because such people are not living from the basis of their own firm beliefs.

The majority of people today seem to think it best simply to imitate what others do, following their lead without giving it any thought of their own. Day after day, many of us put in a great deal of effort, perseverance, and training in order to do what is commonly thought to be 'good,' pushing on without giving it much consideration. We cannot truly uplift ourselves this way, because we are denying the limitless abilities, intuition, and wisdom that firmly reside within us, and are limiting ourselves with the fixed ideas that we have adopted in our heads.

We may be sincere, well-meaning, hardworking people, but if we wish to make manifest the life that we have envisioned and drawn up inside our head, first of all, we need to be aware that our infinite abilities have resided within us from the very start. Our true, pure, genuine self, unaffected and free of falsity, overflowing with infinite wisdom and intuition, has always been inside us. To manifest this original self is our true heart's desire—the true purpose of our life.

For those of us who have been immersed for a long time in the world of common assumptions and conventional thinking, submitting to its control, the steps that we take from here on are of utmost importance. The question is, to what extent will we be able to cast away all the surface knowledge and beliefs that we have accumulated thus far? This, in itself, is the key to attuning ourselves to the universal law.

Reviving the memory of our divine self

I do not mean to negate all that we have learned, acquired, and experienced in the past. Nothing in our life is useless or wasted. The things we have learned are all used in their own ways, each making up a part of the whole. At the same time, we do not need to cling to or get caught up in the past. This is because, by rising above the common assumptions and beliefs that we have held up to now, we begin to recognize and awaken to our infinite potential. The thoughts and experiences we have accumulated in the past are all part of a process that is spurring us toward this awakening, so that we can encounter our true, divine self. Nothing in this world occurs by coincidence. Everything happens for a reason. It is all a process of learning.

For each and every one of us, prayer for world peace offers a sure method for revealing our wonderful, innate qualities and abilities, without relying on an external God, or handing over our authority to others, or shifting our responsibilities onto someone or something else. Through prayer for world peace, we are able to draw out our original infinite abilities to the fullest and create a radiant life for ourselves. At the same time, we are also helping to uplift all of humanity and contributing to the peace of the world.

If we are unable to love ourselves, forgive ourselves, or believe in ourselves, we cannot possibly love others, forgive others, or believe in others. If we are unable to recognize the divinity in ourselves, we cannot possibly affirm the divinity in others. The essence of life lies in giving unlimited expression to the ultimate truth of our inner divinity through our words and actions. If we focus our consciousness on this divine self, everything will fall into place and everything will be perfectly arranged.

And yet, in the process of creating our lives, many of us continue to make choices and decisions based on things that occurred in the past. We determine our future on the basis of unpleasant, bitter memories—memories of failure, despair, and betrayal, memories of being unloved—memories that we would rather not revisit. When making decisions about the future, we recall these memories and think, *I will no longer be deceived. I will no longer be cast aside. I will no longer be betrayed. I will no longer be the loser. Never again will I love. Never will I forgive. Never again will I fail. I won't go down that road again. I won't make that mistake twice. This time will be different*, and so on. We firmly imprint past emotions and past memories in our mind, and when it comes time to make new choices and decisions, these memories and emotions are what come to the fore.

With sentiments like *I never want to do that again, I won't make that mistake twice, I don't want to get hurt,*

and *I don't want to suffer* at the forefront of our consciousness, our "*I don't want to…*" mentality guides
us to make choices and decisions that ultimately bring
us the opposite of the life that we wanted. Although
we know full well that we should not repeat the same
mistaken choices that we made in the past, when the
moment arrives, the memories in our subconscious
override our conscious mind, causing us to unwittingly
make those very same choices again. This happens because our negative past memories have not disappeared
from our mind.

We need to let those memories of the past fade away
and disappear. We need to transform our thought energy
into vibrations of bright light. To do this, the fundamental method that I most often recommend is the prayer
method of *Fading away—May peace prevail on Earth*.

The decisions that we have made up to now may very
well surprise even ourselves. Our unconscious choices are much stronger than our conscious ones, due to
the past memories that have been deeply ingrained and
imprinted in our mind over a long, long period of time.
Because we do not have a deep awareness of this, we
simply act from force of habit and take the same mistaken
road that we did in the past.

This can be said about individuals and about human-kind in general. Although all of humanity dearly wishes for peace, we have unconsciously guided ourselves to war. Everyone wishes to avoid illness, yet we still become ill. We don't want to make the same mistakes again and again, but it often happens that we do. All of these are the results of our unconscious decisions.

If these unconscious choices and decisions are not recognized and redirected toward conscious ones, neither our own lives nor the future of humanity will take a turn for the better. This is why it is so important that each one of us take responsibility for ourselves and endeavor not to be tossed about by our own memories of the past. Instead, we can calmly observe those memories and regard them as phenomena that are appearing in the process of fading away, and cast them into our prayers for world peace.

Each of us needs to recall our original memory—the memory of our true, divine self. The method of *Fading away—May peace prevail on Earth* is here for this purpose. Those who are able to encounter and grasp this deep, expansive, elevated truth are pioneers among humanity, able to freely obtain the infinite happiness and peace they desire. They can do this because each and every human being is equally endowed with infinite capabilities and infinite potential. Through prayer for world peace, we can choose to enter a world free of illness and misfortune.

Originally published in Japanese, April 2006

The Words I Speak

Be conscious of the self who is speaking

The divine mind is infinite love, infinite forgiveness, infinite wisdom, infinite happiness, health, life, power, and light. As we continue to think of peace and pray for peace, this truth comes to resonate through our whole being, and we even surpass the stage of having to think, *I will not allow myself to speak negatively*. The desire to express dark, pessimistic sentiments no longer exists in our mind, and the only topics we speak about are bright, positive ones.

Why is it that we give so much importance to the words we speak? It is because we know that our words create our life. The words we have unconsciously spoken up to now have created the life we are experiencing at present.

In the past, we may have spoken to others in a routine manner, saying things like, "I see what you mean," or "No, you're wrong." But before we say "you," we first need to be conscious of our own *self*, the 'I' who is speaking. We need to confirm which self is speaking. We need to make sure that it is not our former self—the self who lived and behaved out of force of habit—but the self who manifests our inner divine nature.

And so, from here on, I would like to ask that before sending out any words, you consciously remind yourself: *I myself am the one who is speaking these words.* When we speak with an awareness of our divine self—our divine mind—and steadily maintain this awareness, careless words will cease to slip out of our mouths. Only good, positive words will naturally flow forth.

Just think about it. Does the divine mind speak negative words? Does the divine mind speak of illness, suffering, sorrow, or discontent? The divine mind never speaks of such things. The divine mind speaks only radiant words, filled with love, forgiveness, and light.

If we deeply and firmly wish to, we can definitely speak from our divine mind at all times. All we need to do is practice. Before uttering any words, let's take a deep breath and consciously think to ourselves, *I am a divine life. My divine self is sending out words. My divine self is speaking to the divine being in the other person.*

Up to now, we may have been using our words quite casually, paying little or no attention to the 'I' who is speaking. But from here on, we can make a new start. With our spouse, our partner, our children, our friends, and everyone in our lives, we can begin to speak with conscious attention, always taking the standpoint of our essential, divine self.

For a long time, we may have spoken from the standpoint of an 'I' who clings to the past, who is stuck in commonplace thinking and fixed ideas, who is dissatisfied, who passes judgment on everything, and who sees this world as a miserable place. But now it is time to absolutely sever this habit. Now it is time to consciously speak from our divine mind. Even when another person throws negative words at us, even when we are blamed or hated, our divine self replies in a way that sees the other person as a divine being, acknowledging only their good points.

If we stop and think about why the other person is speaking to us so negatively, we realize that it's because they themselves are suffering in some way—in pain, sadness, or distress. This is what leads them to be at odds with us. It is an expression of their wounded ego. Once we understand this, we are able to forgive the person. This forgiving self is our divine self.

When our divine self speaks, no negative words come out, because our divine self acknowledges the divine being in the other person. Our divine self never sees the other person as unclean, unsightly, tarnished, or sinful. Our divine self sees only the person's most wonderful aspects.

Our past self may have been constantly worried about pain, sorrow, illness, or being laid off. Our lives may have been almost wholly governed by pre-existing habits, and we may have been quick to blame and judge others. Then, when standing before a celebrated or powerful person, we may have put ourselves down, seeing ourselves as foolish and incompetent. But this past self is not the real you or the real me. It is not our essential, divine self.

The past has no power

I believe that the vast majority of people are still holding on to the past. Almost everyone is holding on to past difficulties, sorrows, pain, and resentment.

However, we need to know that the events of the past will not come leaping into the present. Past events and incidents are done and gone. Any mistake that we made, any time when we were mistreated, any pain, sadness, or regrettable incident—none of them will barge in on our present self and bring our life to a standstill. There is no power in the past.

Any past difficulty, sorrow, pain, or distress, whether related to a thing, an idea, or an incident, has no power of its own—none whatsoever. We are the ones who are giving it power. When we recall those past ideas, events, and incidents, and hold them tightly within us, we are giving our life-power to them. By calling forth the memory of past events and past emotions, we are re-creating our own unhappiness.

No incident from the past can have any power or do us any harm if we do not direct our thoughts toward it. The past has no power whatsoever to interfere with or spoil either our present reality or our future. No matter how others may have given us trouble in the past, those past events no longer have any power of their own.

Why, then, are we still hurting? It is because, when we close our eyes to our true identity—our innate divine self—we inevitably remain caught up in the pain, resentment, envy, and bitterness that we tasted in the past. And in clutching at those past events again and again, we continue to give power to them.

No matter what kind of terribly bitter or painful experiences we may have had in the past, not one of them has the power to bring harm to us now. Not a single one. This is why people who have let go of their past are immediately able to start creating a new future.

All of the pain, sorrow, strife, religious conflict, ethnic and cultural discrimination, and killing that humanity has suffered arose from things that took place in the past. If everyone stopped clutching at the past, all that would exist are the present and the future. Up to now, the majority of humanity has not realized this. Yet, all of us have the ability to grasp this truth. We are all capable of recognizing that within us we hold a power great enough to change the fate of this earth. How can this be possible? It becomes possible when we catch hold of our divine self. When we catch hold of our divine self we are residing in a higher dimension than we did before, and accessing a tremendous creative power far greater than anything we could have imagined.

Divine words have a purifying power

In the past, we may have sent out all sorts of words. But from here on, we will speak words not of the past, but of the present. Through our own present words, we will be purifying the words we sent out in the past. And at the same time, we will be transforming all of humanity's dark, negative words into vibrations of light. When we speak, our divine self will speak—not our past self that was spiteful, resentful, fiercely competitive, or egoistic.

When our ego is present, we talk endlessly about "me, me, me," constantly pointing out our own value and importance. But from now on, the 'I' who speaks will not be the 'I' with a great career, the 'I' with amazing abilities, or the 'I' who thinks highly of ourselves. It will not be the 'I' who was born into material wealth, or who looks at the differences between oneself and others. The 'I' who speaks now is the divine 'I'—the 'I' who loves deeply, who forgives all, who shines radiantly. The words spoken by this 'I' are the words that will create a new future.

Please stop and take a moment to praise yourself for having come to this point. It is so very important to praise ourselves for our sincere efforts and shining qualities, because if we cannot praise and love ourselves, we cannot love others, either.

Of course, taking pride in ourselves does not mean feeling superior about our career, the difficult exams we have passed, the prestige we have achieved, or other ways in which we have excelled compared to others. That kind of boastfulness belongs to a past self—a competitive, egoistic self, a self who no longer exists.

As an example, seeking to wear brand name clothes and admiring them above all else is not an activity of our divine self. Rather, it is an expression of our ego— something that makes us feel superior to others. That kind of egoism no longer exists within us. But the moment we draw our past closer to us again, recalling the clothes we used to wear, or this handbag or that house or the outstanding abilities we used to exhibit, and talking about them, we are once again giving our thought-energy to the past. Then, we again become embroiled in thoughts filled with envy and criticism. Our ego takes joy in picking out the shortcomings of others. When we re-enliven those kinds of thoughts and behavior, we are going right back to the past.

If we deeply wish to free ourselves from all traces of an egoistic consciousness, we can look for suitable ways to train ourselves. The most fundamental self-training method that I recommend is the method of *Fading away—May peace prevail on Earth* that was introduced by my mentor and adoptive father, Masahisa Goi (see Appendices I and II). Also, thousands of divine-minded people have taken great strides by making silent affirmations to remind themselves of their innate divine nature. Another effective practice is to repeat words of gratitude and other bright, encouraging words in our minds—as well as reciting them aloud or writing them down while holding our breath.[7] Deep breathing methods and other exercises can also be powerful ways to train ourselves while sparking a divine reawakening throughout humanity as a whole. (Please see the appendices for information on some of the practices that I recommend. For further ideas, please refer to my book *Essentials of Divine Breathing*.)

Whatever self-training practices we may adopt, I feel that it is essential to always use words that affirm our own divine nature as well as the divine nature of the earth, the universe, and all that exists. If our practice focuses only on our individual self, without a spirit of reverence for the divine universe and all living beings, I do not think it will enable us to truly connect with our inner divine nature.

And even if we don't undertake any self-training practices, there is one simple way to keep our minds on a high plane. All we need to do is take a moment before speaking and consciously think of our divine self. It takes only a fraction of a second. If we are living consciously, we can do it. On the other hand, if we simply continue to live according to habit, it will be very hard for us to find true and lasting peace of mind.

If we truly wish to experience the joy of living, we must refrain from holding on to the past. We must refrain from giving power to the past. We human beings become unhappy when we give power to past incidents and past negative emotions. In truth, our role is to purify the past, on behalf of all humanity. When we think peace, speak peace, and pray for peace, we are doing so on behalf of humanity. Likewise, when our past thoughts and emotions are purified, similar thoughts and emotions emitting from other people are purified at the same time.

Our divine self cannot be harmed

When we live in this way, we are creating peace on earth. When enough people think peace and speak peace, peace will definitely come to this world. The aim is to see human divinity made manifest. When we speak from our divine self, it means that we recognize the divine nature in all human beings.

From the perspective of our habitual, unconscious self, other people may appear to be full of shortcomings and faults, and we speak to them as such. But when our divine self is speaking, we see the divine being in others, and in ourselves as well. This is the underlying principle behind the steadfast practice of *Fading away—May peace prevail on Earth*. When we say, "It's fading away," we are letting go of our past, unenlightened mindset. We are allowing it to fade away and vanish into nothingness. Whenever something from the past comes up in our minds or in our circumstances, we think to ourselves: *It's faded away! It's gone! With this, everything is sure to get better! How grateful I am!*

Even though the past has disappeared, we might tend to recall those past incidents and feelings again and again. This is why we continue to engage in self-training. We can only be happy when we have trained ourselves to release our hold on the past.

It is vitally important not to give any power to the past. We need to understand in our head why the past has no power. When we think that it has some power and drag the past out, giving power to it, it is as if we are taking pleasure in repeatedly turning over the past in our mind. We are wasting our energy on something totally pointless.

Before we speak, before we utter even a word, I recommend that we consciously think, *My divine self is speaking. The person before me is a divine being.* However, it often happens that the person we are speaking to is not yet aware of this. Although this person is originally a divine life, they may still be preoccupied with the past and say all kinds of unreasonable, unfair things. But our divine self can think, *Saying these insulting things to me is part of this person's path to manifesting their own divine nature.*

The divine mind is pure love, and thus, whatever thoughts other people might send out, the divine mind absorbs them and transforms them into light. Therefore, our divine self is unharmed by anything. People might bombard us with violent words and behavior that have nothing to do with us, but our divine self will not be harmed. This is because our divine self exists on a much higher plane than that. Whatever destructive energy comes our way, whatever illness or difficulty we are handed, our divine self remains unaffected. This is the power of the divine mind: our deep knowledge of our essential, divine nature enables us to transform any situation into light.

If, on the other hand, we assimilate with the negative energy that is being projected, the pathogen that brought about someone else's illness is likely to make us sick as well. There is no need to take in those kinds of discordant, emotional thoughts. All we need to do is to keep emitting light. All we need to do is to keep thinking and speaking words that bring others happiness. When we do, happiness is promised for us, too.

Our ultimate joy in life

From here on, we will continue changing at a quick pace, and the life that we envision will open up for us. It absolutely will.

From today on, the words that we utter will be the words of our divine self, and the person we speak to will draw out their own divine nature. When you speak to someone, please do your best to see their good points. When you do, the brilliant light of peace will shine all around you, and your heart will be filled with peace.

You may have family who, as they live in society, still

experience pain, sadness, or envy over what they are lacking. But when they sense how your heart is filled with peace, they, too, will naturally start to make changes in their thinking.

We have now reached a point where we can think, *My existence is light itself and divinity itself.* If the words we speak from now on are indeed the words of our divine mind, then our divine nature will become manifest before long. Our prayers for peace set the stage for this.

With this kind of consciousness, together we will construct a world at peace. This, I feel, is our ultimate joy in life. Therefore, at all times, let us speak to others with words that make them joyful.

Originally published in Japanese, June 2010
Adapted from a talk given in February 2010

Quest for the Self

One time in my life, I was swept away with a feeling of love and the desire to tightly embrace every single human being in this world, without exception. I felt this power of love—a power that transcends all—rise up within me, condense, and spread out to the ends of the universe.

Even now, this moment comes vividly back to mind. Suddenly, and to a surprising degree, the power of love flowed out from inside me and erupted. It was a mysterious power, brimming with sacred wisdom.

That was the moment when I awoke to my heavenly mission.

Seeking out the divine within us

Creating peace on earth and happiness for all humanity means searching for and pursuing the divine qualities that reside within each one of us. It is not about pursuing pain, misfortune, and sorrow. These are utterly useless pursuits, yet how much time have we already thrown away on them?

The mission bestowed on each and every human being is simply this: to seek out and give recognition to the divine being within us. When we have grasped this profound universal truth, we know that every last human being, no matter how they might appear on the surface, is divinity itself—a noble, sacred, radiantly shining being.

This is not a concept or theory. When our inner soul encounters this truth, the anxieties, afflictions, pain, and sorrow that we are holding on to all disappear, and we become aware of the immeasurable value of human existence in this world.

In the moment of awakening that I described above, I affirmed that all the people in the world are meant to be released from the restrictive thoughts and emotions that we are tightly gripping in our mind. We are meant to bring out our inner divinity, and attain unconditional happiness. Human existence transcends the sufferings and tragedies of the past. All of humanity is governed by a radiant, mystical, infinite light—a truly sacred light, abounding in infinite wisdom.

What determines our fate?

Conditions of misfortune, suffering, and tragedy are not originally inscribed in human beings. From the outset, only one thing is inscribed in our soul: our essential divine nature. The pain, sorrow, and unhappiness that appear to control our lives are merely creations of the negative thoughts and emotions that we have unconsciously been sending out.

Most of our thoughts and emotions are generated almost unconsciously, and even our most trivial, everyday thoughts can influence our surroundings and give shape to our life. Through this process, we are visited by happiness, joy, and serenity, and we also suffer from pain, misfortune, and tragedy. The countless threads spun with the thoughts and emotions that each of us sends out in the course of our daily life form a tapestry that depicts the course our life will take. Even tiny, trivial thoughts pile up and pile up, until they find expression in some incident or event. As this process is repeated over and over, our future course becomes more and more clearly inscribed.

In this way, it can be said that all human beings are bound by the fate we have created by means of our own subconscious mind. At all times, the human subconscious is underlain by negative thoughts and emotions— thoughts of anxiety, distrust, doubt, and so on. Our hearts and minds are snatched away and drawn toward darkness and negativity. We become caught up in this negative side, until all our time is taken up with it. Even now, many of us remain convinced that ideas about humanity's essential goodness, divinity, and light are mere theories and have nothing to do with us.

The tendency that human beings have of latching onto tragedy and misfortune prevents us from readily accepting our true nature—our noble mind, our sacred soul, and our selfless feelings of love. The time that we spare to develop this side of ourselves is almost nil. But the truth is that each and every one of us is furnished with a beautiful, pure, noble, and sacred consciousness.

The path of self-inquiry

As human beings, we must all seek out the meaning and purpose of our lives. Our first step is to consider what kind of quest is most essential for us.

No matter how many times we might pursue suffering, or tragedy, or misfortune, or setback, or failure, these pursuits are meaningless. Or rather, the more we go on pursuing this negative side of ourselves, the more our thoughts become pegged to negative karmic vibrations, until finally we are unable to disentangle ourselves from those unharmonious circumstances.

Such pursuits are not worth the energy that we devote to them. Instead, what each and every one of us should be pursuing is our own self. For as long as we neglect this quest for our self, we cannot bring good, wonderful, radiant things into our life.

In short, the question is, what is the best way for us to live in order to fulfill our heavenly mission for this lifetime? To what use should we put our life? To what should we devote ourselves? The discernment, understanding, and spirit of inquiry that we need to answer these questions are precious qualities indeed.

Moving beyond self-sacrifice

Generally, devoting or sacrificing one's life is seen as admirable behavior, signifying a truly noble spirit. Although it is noble to offer one's life, it poses the question: to what are we devoting ourselves? What are we living (or dying) for? To offer our precious life—our noble life, through which we are meant to fulfill our heavenly mission—through self-sacrifice may seem like an attractive thing to do, but it may indicate that we are still in the process of searching for our self.

For example, let's say you are being stalked by someone. In your fear and anxiety, you sense that your life is in danger, and in an act of self-defense you spontaneously murder the stalker. After that, you are tortured by the thought that you have killed another person, and you long to find an opportunity to atone for it. Then one day, you rescue someone who is in grave danger, and in doing so you lose your own life.

When we sacrifice ourselves for others in this way, out of a desire for atonement, it means that our search for our self is still incomplete. When our self-inquiry deepens to the point that we reach the sacred and divine realm that permeates and surrounds all humankind, we will see that rashly throwing away our precious life without a deeper understanding of our actions is something that goes against our true will. This is because such behavior is the result of things we have said and done in the past, including our previous lifetimes. When our self-inquiry is complete, each and every one of us will be able to sever this baggage that we carry from the past. We will do so by means of our inner quest, and by the invincible belief that we develop as a result.

At present, however, the vast majority of humanity applauds self-sacrifice as a virtuous and admirable act. And indeed, there are some acts of self-sacrifice that truly inspire others and give them courage. But all of us can rise above self-sacrifice, to a way of living that is even more elevated, noble, and sublime.

With deeper self-inquiry, there is no self-sacrifice

What I mean here by 'self-sacrifice' is offering ourselves for the sake of others by means of our physical death. However, the mindset that praises and admires this kind of sacrifice makes it very difficult for humanity to guide itself toward its ultimate, elevated state of divine awareness. Rather, what it does is to define a self-sacrificial death as a fixed point that humanity is meant to reach, and this prevents us from going any deeper into ourselves. Because of this, many people are forever unable to reach their ultimate goal of manifesting their divine self.

Those who have beautifully carried out their own inner quest are unmistakably aware of their divine self. For this reason, they never give up on solving a problem, or abandon it halfway. By elevating and drawing forth their infinite wisdom, infinite ability, and infinite intuition, they find solutions to problems and exhibit a way of living in tune with the truth that we are all originally radiant, divine beings.

Those who have awoken to the truth of their own divinity and the divine nature of all humanity are people who did not stop midway, at the stage of self-sacrifice, but instead continue walking straight ahead toward the aim of accomplishing their heavenly mission for this lifetime.

Uplifting both ourselves and others

If we give the highest praise to acts of self-sacrifice, people who are unclear about their purpose in life might be induced to make it their goal to sacrifice themselves. As a result, they might neglect the self-inquiry that should be our most important priority, and might end their lives prematurely, attracting conditions that invite self-sacrifice and never moving beyond that aim.

To accomplish a radiant physical lifetime on earth means to devote ourselves to the happiness of humanity. It is far more difficult a task to uplift humanity while we remain alive than it is to offer ourselves by means of our physical death. And yet, it is also a far nobler way of living, one that is closer to the realm of the divine. Demonstrating the value of our life while we are alive is a much higher hurdle to clear than doing so by means of our death.

If we are holding a latent desire to sacrifice our life for others, and often entertain that kind of thought in our mind, it could end up leading us toward a corresponding outcome. Although sacrificing oneself is indeed a deeply moving act, acts of sacrifice that take place without true understanding are not in tune with our divine nature and with the universal law. In the ultimate sense, I feel, the best way to offer ourselves for the sake of others is to do so in a way that uplifts both them and us. If other lives are spared at the expense of our own life, that in itself does not necessarily mean that our action reflects the divine will.

The heavenly mission that has been given to us for

this lifetime is none other than to inquire into and pursue our true self. It is to dig deeply within ourselves and ask questions like *Who and what am I? What is the purpose of my life? Why do I exist here and now?* As each and every member of humanity carries out this inquiry, we will surge forward on a path to an elevated, sacred world, until finally, we arrive at our divine self.

Historically, there have been divine-minded people who sacrificed their own lives for the sake of humanity, but in these cases, it was their heavenly mission to do so, and their actions were in accordance with the universal divine will. However, for the majority of people today, I do not feel that this kind of sacrifice will truly uplift our soul and manifest our divine nature.

In my view, self-sacrifice is a form of suffering under a different name—one that makes it seem more appealing. But there is absolutely no need for us to make suffering the goal of our life, to attract suffering into our life, or to force ourselves to sacrifice our life for the sake of others.

A way of life that meets the divine mind

It is the will of the universal divine mind and the intention of the various angels, or divinities, to see all of us share in each other's happiness and enjoy radiant lives. The divine mind never wishes for us to use another's misfortune, death, or sacrifice as a stepping-stone to our own happiness.

Likewise, in parent-child relationships, parents are meant to share in the sense of abundance, freedom, intuition, innocence, and limitless potential that their children possess, and children are meant to share in their parents' sense of confidence, their deep, selfless love, and the resilient heart that they have developed through various experiences and emotions. Parents must never make themselves victims of their children, and children must never become their parents' victims.

To truly live means to mutually pursue happiness, joy, and truth, and to share in them as well. It means getting to know ourselves as deeply as we can. This way of living is not limited to parents and children, but applies uniformly to all human relationships.

Before we dedicate our life entirely to someone else, we need to live for ourselves. We need to know the preciousness and dignity of our own life. Before we give up our own aims for the sake of another, we must experience a deep desire to know ourselves and look deeply into ourselves.

Only when we have first uplifted ourselves can we

begin to uplift others. And at the same time, we need to uplift others so that we ourselves can continue being uplifted. Before we can make others happy, we must make ourselves happy, and we must make others happy in order to go on being happy ourselves.

Before anything else, we need to inquire into our own truth and acknowledge that we are an expression of divinity itself. And in order to remain connected with our inner, divine truth, we need to carry out acts that recognize the divine nature in others.

Thus, the ultimate aim for all human beings is to know our true self. By inquiring deeply into ourselves, we arrive at the truth of our divinity, and then we come to recognize the divine nature of all humanity. If we sacrifice ourselves without knowing our true self, it will not lead to true deliverance for anyone. This is because it is only by recognizing the divine nature of all human beings that we can know what others truly need.

If we cannot make ourselves happy, not only will we be burdened with sorrow and grief, but we will spread that sorrow and grief to others. A child's pain is also the parents' pain, and a parent's sadness is also their children's sadness. Happiness and peace are never the work of one person alone.

Accepting the principle of *fading away*

It is through our relationships with others that our life takes shape. Over the course of our lifetime, we encounter all kinds of people. Whether our connections with those people are positive or negative, our life is greatly influenced by the ways in which we receive and respond to the various phenomena that we experience.

As our inner quest progresses and deepens, we become able to transcend all the good and evil from our past, and our life blossoms magnificently.

In the past, when we were not conducting any self-inquiry, we were filled with prejudice and distorted views, and our greed, baseness, and weakness led us to react with fear and anxiety to the various phenomena that manifested before us. We could not prepare to accept these phenomena as our own. If we cannot accept these phenomena, they might cease for a while, but similar occurrences are likely to repeat themselves again and again until we are able to understand the true meaning of *fading away* (see Appendices I and II).

The *fading away* process gives us much-needed lessons and experiences. What is our connection with this incident or circumstance? What are we meant to learn, what are we meant to experience, what are we meant to accomplish? There is no meaning to any of it if the two parties involved do not move beyond their current stage by recognizing that the phenomenon is appearing in order to reveal itself and then fade away and vanish forever. On the other hand, if both parties accept this fading away process as a means of revealing their inner divine self, then the whole thing will disappear in an instant. Through profound truth, wisdom, and elevated thoughts, both parties can gain a thorough understanding of what this phenomenon means for them. And immediately, both will rise up to a higher place.

Alternatively, suppose one party involved in the incident has already purified and elevated their thoughts, while the other is still mired in wickedness. In this case, too, the same incident or circumstance can embrace both parties and lift them up together to a more elevated state as it appears and then vanishes away.

Every person who appears throughout our lifetime—whether kindhearted or malicious, hateful or loving, an enemy or an ally, a competitor or a partner, a husband or wife, parent or child, brother or sister, or simply a passerby—appears in accordance with causes that we generated during previous lifetimes. We can freely draw these encounters toward us in a way that corresponds with our own process of self-inquiry, at the most suitable time and place, in the most suitable form, and with the involvement of the most suitable people for our present self.

The basic outline for this present lifetime was constructed during our previous lifetimes and cannot be totally circumvented, but depending on the way we receive and respond to the various events and incidents that take place, there is plenty of potential to alter their conditions, circumstances, and outcomes. It all depends on the degree of our self-inquiry. And so, the end results of the various *fading away* phenomena that we encounter can vary widely.

The *fading away* process conveys to us the truth that every person who appears before us throughout our life is a divine being. The suffering, resentment, hatred, unhappiness, and tragedy that may be brought on by others take a variety of forms depending on our relationships with those people. For this reason, it is imperative that we do not focus on other people's untruths and wrongdoings, nor on the various unhappy circumstances that come about through their actions. Rather than getting caught up in the emotions connected with these external phenomena, we need to look within ourselves for our inner truth.

Self-inquiry is not the same as self-analysis, nor does it mean judging ourselves by measuring the good and evil within us. Self-inquiry is synonymous with the well-known phrase *Know thyself*. What is meant by 'thyself' in this phrase? It is our essential, divine self.

Our life is a journey on which we search deeply within ourselves to arrive at this divine self-awareness. It is a path that we all must take, one that cannot be avoided. And its end goal is one that every one of us absolutely must arrive at.

When we look deeply into ourselves and come to understand our essential divine nature, we no longer have anything to be afraid of. All the phenomena that appear in our life are created by our own mind, or else jointly with those connected with us. Thus, if we firmly grasp the truth of human divinity and make it our own, our mind will no longer generate any negative phenomena. At the same time, we will become aware of how many negative phenomena our mind used to create in the past.

All of the new phenomena that we create will be happy, peaceful, harmonized phenomena that bring joy to all people. That is all we will generate from here on.

Life is creation.

Life is joy.

Life is a process through which we and others awaken to and arrive at our ultimate truth.

From here on, the lives that we create will be the genuine creations of divine-minded people.

All experiences are equally precious

In actuality, there is no difference at all between good experiences and bad experiences—all experiences are equal. Although all of us human beings learn various things through our experiences, we should not judge or assess those experiences as good or bad.

By what standard do we judge our own experiences and the experiences of others? The answer is that there is no reason to judge them at all. Why is this? It's because even if a certain experience is presently thought to be bad or negative, through that experience, we are preparing to learn truth. In that regard, any experience that helps to directly connect us with truth cannot be a bad experience.

We human beings tend to make judgments about what is good or bad based solely on surface phenomena and outward appearances. But is there any validity to these judgments? No, there is not. All our experiences are equally valuable. Despite the arbitrary decisions we might make that a certain experience was good or bad, without fail, all our experiences are part of a process through which we are guided toward our true self.

No matter what kinds of experiences we may have had, it will not do us any good to put one experience above another or to make judgments or valuations, let alone regard any experience with contempt. Even if we take pride in being a good and virtuous person, there is no telling when, having become entangled in some sort of external circumstance, we might find ourselves drifting astray.

Throughout our life, until the moment we die, we cannot make judgments about what is good or bad. All of us undergo a multitude of experiences, one after another, in the process of searching for truth and searching for our self.

The role of divine-minded people

For those who have awakened to their divine consciousness, the remaining years will bring only happy, peaceful, light-filled experiences. But at the same time, we must never make judgments about the experiences of others. If this kind of activity is taking place in our mind, it means that we have not yet fully arrived. More and more, we need to keep polishing and elevating our mind and transcend all discriminatory notions and judgments of good and bad that come from our old, misguided thought-habits.

Our new approach to life begins with the people closest to us. Our divine self must come alive in our interactions with our spouse or partner, our parents and children, our brothers and sisters, and our friends and acquaintances. It will not do to simply keep truth in our mind as an idea or concept. It is not the real thing unless we manifest it through actual experience. As divine-minded people, it is our role to demonstrate the ultimate truth of our divinity in our interactions with others.

We will never judge others.

We will never look down on others.

We will never blame others.

We will never badmouth others.

We will never discriminate against others.

We will see all people as divine beings.

We will forgive all people.

We will embrace all people.

We will accept all people.

We will be thankful toward all people.

We will love all people.

When we are able to treat all people—all of humanity—as divine beings, at that time, all of our restraints from the past will have evaporated.

Becoming infinitely more loving

At the time when I discovered the noble, beautifully shining resources within myself, I realized that these very same resources exist within everyone. This was not an idea or concept that I had, but something I truly felt and experienced.

Unless we first make ourselves people of deep love, beauty, and dignity, there is no way we can uplift others and help light the way for them to unlock these abundant resources. If we ourselves do not experience this radiance, splendor, and abundance in ourselves, how can we hope to be aware of these same qualities in others? My heart is filled with love, reverence, and gratitude for each and every member of humanity. If I am uplifted, others will be uplifted at the same time. And as people's divine understanding continues to develop, it will become possible for new, more profound truths to be introduced into this world.

At all times, I am working to infinitely elevate the love that I am pouring into humanity. This love must not be a love of sympathy, pity, or consolation. I am praying with the aim of a noble, elevated, and utterly pure divine love—a love that transcends emotion and embodies truth itself—a ray of light from the universal divine mind. Through divine love, all people can rise above the pain and sorrow of acts like self-sacrifice, and merge into the love of the universal divine mind.

Now, in the 21st century, it is possible for all humanity to attain a pure and absolute kind of love—not a love based on sympathy, aid, or guidance, such as when people respond to the tragedy of self-sacrifice, but an unconditional, completely selfless love. For this purpose, let us continue praying for world peace while uplifting ourselves and others.

Originally published in Japanese, August 2001

Notes

1. Adapted from an uncredited translation on www.eastoftheweb.com.

2. Masahisa Goi (1916-1980) was a Japanese philosopher who started an international movement of prayer for world peace. He is the author of numerous books on the subject of spiritual development and world peace. Masahisa Goi was the mentor of Masami Saionji, and became her adoptive father when he designated her as his spiritual successor. He is commonly referred to as 'Goi Sensei' (in Japanese, *sensei* means 'teacher).

3. For more about guardian divinities and guardian spirits, please refer to *God and Man* by Masahisa Goi.

4. Excerpted from *God and Man* by Masahisa Goi.

5. Thinking positive thoughts to counter negative words or thoughts is part of the practice of light-filled thinking advocated by the author. For more about this practice, please see Appendix III.

6. Rupert Sheldrake is a British author, speaker, and researcher. He is best known for his concept of 'morphic resonance,' which hypothesizes that natural systems (such as a species or a type of molecule) possess a collective memory that is inherited from previous similar systems and is passed along to others, as a kind of biological habit. 'Morphic fields' are the fields in which morphic resonance takes place, allowing members of a group to connect and influence each other without direct interaction. For more information, visit Dr. Sheldrake's website at www.sheldrake.org.

7. Writing bright words and phrases in tune with our breathing is one of the ways of creating handwritten mandalas. For more on this practice, please visit EarthHealersHandbook.net. Masami Saionji's books *Think Something Wonderful* and *Essentials of Divine Breathing* also offer practical exercises that readers may find useful.

APPENDICES

The Practice of *Fading Away—May Peace Prevail on Earth*

When we find ourselves swept up in dark, negative energy, how can we dispel that negative feeling and restore our original, essential spirit of harmony, gratitude, and love?

The method I most often recommend is one that I learned from my adoptive father and mentor, Masahisa Goi. The method works like this: When a dark or discordant thought, such as fear or resentment, passes through our mind, we respond to it mentally with the words *Fading away—May peace prevail on Earth*. Whenever something unpleasant occurs within us or around us, we say these words to ourselves, as many times as we wish.

The principle behind this method is that the various

thoughts and emotions we have, as well as the circumstances that arise in our lives, are not being newly created now, nor did they appear out of nowhere. Rather, they are manifestations of thoughts that we first created a long, long time ago—a time that we may no longer remember. They are emerging now in our surface consciousness, or else in the circumstances that surround us, in order to fade away and vanish forever.

In order to let them disappear, we have to let go of them. We must not cling to them or get upset by them. All we have to do is let them fade away, and replace them with a bright, divinely-inspired thought such as *May peace prevail on Earth*.

Fading away—May peace prevail on Earth. We can repeat these words to ourselves while we are sitting, standing, walking, working, exercising, or relaxing—anytime at all. If we find it hard to concentrate on the words, we can try repeating them as we are naturally inhaling and exhaling, or while holding our breath. The important thing is to continue practicing this method over and over again, without giving up. (For ideas on how to practice this method in tune with our breathing, refer to my book *Essentials of Divine Breathing*.)

By using this method day after day, we can absolutely make a change in our thought-habits. With daily practice, we can convert all our energy back to the energy of love. Finally, before we know it, we will discover that we have re-connected with our original nature as divine beings and direct embodiments of love.

When we become direct embodiments of love, we never experience fear, and all our energy is activated toward the positive. That is when we naturally come to understand who we truly are and what life is all about.

— Masami Saionji

Quotes from Masahisa Goi on the Method of *Fading Away— May Peace Prevail on Earth*

If you are practicing the method of *Fading away—May peace prevail on Earth*, you might find it helpful to refer to these quotes from Masahisa Goi, where he talks about the principle behind it. Many people say that reading these quotes helps them to renew their courage and brighten their state of mind. As a result, they are able to practice the 'fading away method' more effectively.

The only real existence is divinity, which is good, truth and love. Everything else is in the process of fading away.

———

Do not get caught up in the past. The past is a vanishing image. It will fade away.

———

Spiritual faith means leaving everything up to divine love. Nothing else needs to be added.

It would be good if you could accept everything that happens around you, thinking, *It's all right. There is a divine meaning underneath it.* This, however, may not be easy to do. So instead, just think that everything, whether good or bad, is fading away, and keep thinking or praying, *May peace prevail on Earth.* Do this all the time, with your whole being. There is no substitute for steady practice.

———

The practice of *fading away* is not something that you do with your willpower. It is not your physical self that extinguishes karma, or sin. Karma is extinguished by the light of your guardian divinity and spirits. Your part in this process is to pray for world peace.

———

When you are praying, your true self is shining brightly. If a variety of thoughts pop into your mind it is nothing to worry about, because those thoughts are nothing more than vanishing images from a past consciousness, emerging in order to disappear. Don't be concerned about them at all. Just keep praying.

———

Here is a good way to think: *Day by day, my old self is fading away. Day by day, I am newly reborn, enlivened by divine light from heaven.*

———

As things occur around you, if you think: *It has vanished! It is gone!* it is the same as letting your inner divine nature shine forth.

———

People who practice spiritual faith must never, ever blame others. They need to have big hearts. Forgive yourself and forgive others. Pray for peace with the certainty that all circumstances emerge in the process of fading away.

———

It is of utmost importance for human beings to free themselves from emotionalism. This does not mean that you should repress your emotions, pushing them deeper into your heart. Nor does it mean that you should vent them in front of other people and disturb their peace of mind. What, then, can you do when turbulent emotions rise within you? Pour them into a prayer for world peace, straightaway. Think that all of your negative emotions are in the process of fading away, and are constantly being transformed into brighter ones through your prayer for world peace. To be able to do this, you need to practice daily.

———

In general, the distinctions people make between good people and bad people, or likable people and dislikable people, are based on their own emotions. They seldom see a truly good person as good. For them, a good person is someone who serves their interests and a bad person is someone who does not. They gauge everything by their own interests.

As long as people keep thinking this way, the world will never be at peace. But since this kind of attitude is difficult to get rid of, what can people do? I suggest that, at the moment when such feelings emerge, we regard them as being in the process of fading away. All occurrences, feelings, thoughts, and circumstances—good and bad alike—should be directed straight into the waves of a world peace prayer, such as *Fading away—May peace prevail on Earth*. Within those waves, all things will be purified by the great divine light that is guiding and protecting humanity.

Practice doing this over and over again, and it should give you a clean, sparkly feeling.

If something undesirable should surface, think intently: *My karma from the past has vanished through this. Things will absolutely get better from now on.*

Your soul is set free when you know that, no matter how great the pain, any and all suffering will absolutely vanish with the passing of time.

—

There is nothing that can bring harm to you from the outside. The only things that can bring harm upon you are your own thoughts and feelings. However, those thoughts are in the process of vanishing away.

—

The practice of *fading away* is something that you do in your own life. It is not meant to be forced on others.

Excerpted from *I Heard It Like This: The Wisdom of Masahisa Goi*, compiled by Hideo Takahashi

Light-Filled Thinking

Today, more and more people are becoming aware that our words and thoughts carry energy that creates our lives and the world around us. We are realizing how important it is to consciously choose even the most casual words that we use in daily life. When we think and speak positive, light-filled words and phrases, their energy lives on forever, radiating light to all humanity, healing people's hearts and spreading happiness and joy.

To think and speak bright, positive words at all times is a matter of changing our habits. However, it takes practice, dedication, and constant awareness.

When a dark thought crosses your mind, counter it with a bright one like *Infinite light!* When you feel gloomy or sullen, banish that feeling with a phrase like *Infinite improvement! Infinite joy!* or *Infinite possibility!*

If you practice this day in and day out, before you know it, you will find that life is taking a brighter direction. Be as creative as you like with your bright words—the possibilities are infinite!

Below are some light-filled expressions that anyone can practice thinking and saying in their daily life. These are only examples, and you are welcome to add to the list and make it your own. *Infinite creativity!*

Infinite Love
Infinite Harmony
Infinite Peace
Infinite Light
Infinite Power
Infinite Wisdom
Infinite Life

May peace prevail on Earth

Infinite Happiness
Infinite Flourishing
Infinite Richness
Infinite Supply
Infinite Success
Infinite Ability
Infinite Possibility

May peace prevail on Earth

Infinite Health
Infinite Radiance
Infinite Healing
Infinite Renewal
Infinite Clarity
Infinite Vitality
Infinite Hope

May peace prevail on Earth

Infinite Freedom
Infinite Creativity
Infinite Expansion
Infinite Expression
Infinite Development
Infinite Growth
Infinite Gratitude

May peace prevail on Earth

Infinite Joy
Infinite Beauty
Infinite Youth
Infinite Goodness
Infinite Sincerity
Infinite Purity
Infinite Integrity

May peace prevail on Earth

Infinite Energy
Infinite Courage
Infinite Progress
Infinite Improvement
Infinite Strength
Infinite Intuition
Infinite Innocence

May peace prevail on Earth

Infinite Forgiveness
Infinite Splendour
Infinite Dignity
Infinite Potential
Infinite Nobleness
Infinite Brightness
Infinite Acceptance

May peace prevail on Earth

Note: For ideas on how to use a variety of bright words, please see *Think Something Wonderful: Exercises in positive thinking* by Masami Saionji.

APPENDIX IV

Gratitude to the Earth and the Environment

In *The Earth Healer's Handbook*, Masami Saionji writes:

*If the earth is to come alive in the 21st century, human-
ity must undergo a great shift in consciousness. Each of us
needs to become aware of the profound relationship that
exists between our thoughts and the health and stability
of the earth. To revive our ailing planet, each of us needs
to infuse the earth with the healing energy of our deep
gratitude for all the earth's blessings.*

*Words of gratitude, thoughts of gratitude, actions of
gratitude toward our beloved earth—as we rekindle this
spirit of gratitude our way of life will naturally change
and the earth will find the power to heal itself... As we*

deepen our sense of oneness with all life on earth, may we each come to know what it truly means to love, cherish, and make the most of our own lives as well.

A simple way that all of us can help to heal and enliven the world of nature—and brighten our own lives at the same time—is to keep sending out words and expressions of love and gratitude to nature. For example, when walking on the earth, we can think or say things like, *Thank you, dear earth! I am so grateful to you for supporting my footsteps!* While drinking a glass of water, we can think, *Dear water, how wonderful you are! How refreshed you make me feel!*

Whether alone or with others, in nature, at home, or anywhere we happen to be, we can offer our gratitude to the earth, the air, the ocean, the mountains, animals, plants, minerals, and anyone or anything else. You are welcome to use these poems just as they are, to modify them as you like, or to create your own and expand the practice even further.

Gratitude to the Earth

We thank the love of the universe
for supporting our lives through the earth.
Beloved earth,
giver of life,
home to all life,
how can we thank you?
May peace prevail on Earth.
On behalf of humanity,
we offer our gratitude
to the earth.

Gratitude to the Ocean

We thank the love of the universe
for sustaining our lives through the ocean.
Deep ocean,
vast ocean,
abundant ocean,
how can we thank you?
May peace prevail on Earth.
On behalf of humanity,
we offer our gratitude
to the ocean.

Gratitude to Mountains

We thank the love of the universe
for purifying our lives with mountains.
Noble mountains,

mystical mountains,
divine mountains,
how can we thank you?
May peace prevail on Earth.
On behalf of humanity,
we offer our gratitude
to the mountains.

Gratitude to Food

We thank the love of the universe
for sustaining our lives with food.
Nourishing food,
precious food,
life-giving food,
how can we thank you?
May peace prevail on Earth.
On behalf of humanity,
we offer our gratitude
to all food.

Gratitude to Water

We thank the love of the universe
for enlivening us with water.
Pure water,
clear water,
flowing water,
how can we thank you?
May peace prevail on Earth.
On behalf of humanity,

we offer our gratitude
to all water.

Gratitude to Animals
We thank the love of the universe
for blessing our lives with animals.
Innocent animals,
affectionate animals,
hardworking animals,
how can we thank you?
May peace prevail on Earth.
On behalf of humanity,
we offer our gratitude
to all animals.

Gratitude to Plants
We thank the love of the universe
for gracing our lives with plants.
Beautiful plants,
joyful plants,
life-giving plants,
how can we thank you?
May peace prevail on Earth.
On behalf of humanity,
we offer our gratitude
to all plants.

(Poems excerpted from *The Earth Healer's Handbook* by Masami Saionji)

APPENDIX V

A Poem of Gratitude to Nature

The following poem was first delivered by Masami Saionji in September 2016, at the World Conservation Congress held by the International Union for Conservation of Nature (IUCN) in Honolulu, Hawaii, USA.

Headquartered in Switzerland, the IUCN is the world's largest and most diverse environmental network, with offices in over 50 countries and 1,300 member organizations. Every four years the IUCN World Conservation Congress meets to set priorities and agree on the Union's work program.

The theme of the 2016 Congress was "Planet at the Crossroads," emphasizing the need to take action now in order to ensure the survival of humanity and life on earth.

Masami Saionji and her husband Hiroo were invited to take part in the Conservation and Spirituality 'Journey,' to share their wisdom and experience with Congress participants and to speak about the Fuji Declaration (see Appendices VI and VII). The Conservation and Spirituality Journey hosted numerous 'Knowledge Cafés,' where small groups gathered to discuss various topics in an intimate setting.

The Saionjis took part in two Knowledge Cafés, titled "Experiences on Conservation and Spirituality" and "Spirituality and Conservation: from Inspiration to Action." They brought with them a large handwritten mandala with expressions of gratitude to water, which was displayed in one of the conference rooms at the Convention Center, and was also used as a centerpiece for the first Knowledge Café, with participants sitting around it. (To learn about handwritten mandalas, please refer to Masami Saionji's book The Earth Healer's Handbook *or the website www.earthhealershandbook.net.)*

At the "Experiences on Conservation and Spirituality" Café, Mrs. Saionji began by leading everyone in a breathing exercise before giving her talk, which ended with a recitation from her original poem, presented on the following pages.

The Blue Earth Is Alive

by Masami Saionji

The blue earth is alive.
The mystical earth is awakening.
Mountains, rivers, and oceans—
All of nature is full of life,
Dancing with beating hearts.
Within them the mind of God is alive.

Even stones, rocks, and minerals
Are slowly and deeply breathing
Even if we cannot see it with our eyes.
I clearly find God
Shining in such places.

Animals, plants, and fishes, even small insects are active,
Overflowing with the joyful vibrations of God.

The sky is clear and pure
And the sun shines all around.
The land is at ease.

Our bodies and all our cells are shining,

All beings are living together in harmony,
Emitting the light of life.

This is how the planet Earth is meant to be.
But what is the reality on Earth today?

How long has it been since all peoples and nations
Cried out to protect our environment?

Through humanity's self-serving greed,
The Earth has been severely damaged,
The continuation of the species has been endangered,
And we have pursued a path to ruin.
We human beings, each and every one of us, have
    broken our agreement with nature.
We are destroying ecosystems
And bringing harm to one precious life after another.
Now, each of us, all of us, must admit to our wrongdoing.
Fellow human beings, is this the way it should be?
Is this the way we should leave it?
Now, each and every one of us must stand up,
Equally bearing the Earth's heavy burden
And fulfilling our responsibility.

No further can any of us continue our assault on the
Earth.

From here on, we walk a path not of destruction, but of
creation.

No longer has any of us the right to plunder that which
sustains life,

That which the Earth has infinitely and freely supplied.

Fellow human beings, the time has come to wake up.

For those newly born, our posterity,

We can no longer snatch away the resources needed for
life.

The time has come

To ask the sick and damaged Earth to forgive us

And to repay its favors.

Fellow human beings,

As soon as possible, let us ask the Earth for forgiveness,

Unite our hearts one and all,

And, with infinite gratitude, offer ourselves to the Earth.

The time is now.

If we let it pass, no solution is in sight.

Now is the time for all human beings to awaken to the
tremendous blessings freely given by our planet.

On behalf of all humanity, let us offer gratitude to the
    Earth.

Gratitude to the Earth is the wholehearted awareness of
    each and every one of us.
Healing the Earth is the sincere atonement of each and
    every one of us.
Harmonizing the Earth is the deep love of each and
    every one of us.
Bringing peace to the Earth is the heartfelt joy of each
    and every one of us.
Shining on the Earth is the genuine awakening of each
    and every one of us.

Dear planet Earth, please accept our penitence,
Forgive our arrogance and self-serving behavior.
At long last, all humanity will be ashamed of our
    ignorance
And shift to a higher dimensional consciousness.

The planet Earth is one living, evolving entity.
No longer will any human being hinder its evolution.
No longer will any human being destroy its harmony.

Today, earthly humanity is returning to its true self.

We are awakening to our innate sacred consciousness.

We hear the footsteps of a spiritual civilization,

And here today, a new path is dawning.

The Earth, newly revived,

Moves forward along with humanity on a path of
    evolution and self-creation.

The glory of planet Earth is here!

Infinite Gratitude to the Earth!

Note: To learn about handwritten mandalas, please refer to Masami Saionji's book The Earth Healer's Handbook *or the website* **earthhealershandbook.net**.

Introducing the Fuji Declaration

An open letter from Masami Saionji

*The following open letter was issued by Masami Saionji prior to the launching of the Fuji Declaration in May 2015. The Fuji Declaration was co-initiated by Dr. Ervin Laszlo (Founder and President, The Club of Budapest), Mr. Hiroo Saionji (President, The Goi Peace Foundation), and Ms. Masami Saionji (Chairperson, The Goi Peace Foundation). For further information, kindly visit **fujideclaration.org**.*

From moment to moment, the world is relentlessly changing. No one can stop changes from taking place. The question is, in what direction are these changes taking us? Are they opening doorways to a wondrous future, or are they driving us toward ruin and devastation?

During the 20th century, this world experienced a rapid development in material culture and civilization. However, due to the dominance of materialistic values, and the priority given to economic expansion, humanity has been following an extremely dangerous path.

Until now, almost everyone has been striving to lay their hands on limited material resources—resources that are in short supply. Rather than drawing out the infinite resources within us, most of us have set our sights on materialistic aims—physical comforts that will make our life more agreeable. Money, land, houses, cars, delicious things to eat; position, fame, control over others—for a great many people, aims like these are seen as the ultimate reason for living.

Because our thinking is rooted in a belief in limitation, we have created a way of life where everything is lacking: a lack of food, a lack of money, a lack of health, a lack of friendship, a lack of love. Now, all over the world, we can see the results of this way of living. We can see widespread poverty, illness, greed, catastrophes, and environmental destruction. And with each passing day, these conditions are growing more and more severe.

Why is there so much suffering? Why is there so much discrimination, so much mistrust and discontent? All this, I believe, results from our belief in limitation. In struggling with each other to gain limited benefits, we adopted the rule of 'survival of the fittest' and let ourselves be controlled by it. Divisions arose between the winners and the losers, the weak and the strong, the rich and the poor. Those who could grasp the largest share of goods could enjoy a life of ease, while others were left empty-handed. And even when we attained more material benefits than we could ever use, we lived in constant fear of losing them.

Our abuse of great nature has brought us to where the earth is in danger of losing its existence. What are we to do? At this late date, how can we change direction?

Some people feel that we can change the world by tackling each problem and remedying the tangible conditions one by one. Yet unless we make a fundamental change in the mindset that gave rise to them, the same conditions will surely emerge again.

How, then, can we change our underlying attitudes? How can we re-enliven our own hearts? Our only choice, I feel, is to return to our starting point and begin again. We have to search deeply within us to find what is lasting and real.

First, I feel, we need to stop and reflect on what it is that each human heart holds dear. We often hear people call for their rights, demanding freedom and equality. Yet of what value are freedom and equality unless we use them well? We must wake up and see that, sooner or later, we will have to take responsibility for the results of all our decisions—all that we have said and done.

To live responsibly, first and foremost, each of us needs to know the dignity of our own precious life. This, I feel, is our starting point. And when we can sense the dignity of our own life, inevitably, we will hold a feeling of awe toward the lives of others. Today, most of us have forgotten this feeling of awe, respect, and love. Most are still dominated by fear and selfishness. For most, the guiding thought is *As long as I am all right, nothing else matters.*

The hostility, discrimination, chaos and greed that overrun this world all come from the same source—a loss of reverence for the lives of others. Here and now, each human being needs to make a new start and begin caring about the future of humanity. Each human being needs to take just one step forward. It need not be a big step—just something we are capable of. From the moment we take that first step, our lives will start to change. Step by step, doubt will be supplanted by trust, grudges will turn into forgiveness, discrimination will transform into respect, and hostility into conciliation.

We are no longer living in an era where it is sufficient to feel at peace with our own selves. From now on, each and every individual has to join together in affirming the dignity of life. What I suggest is to bring the world's people together with a global-scale charter that transcends all differences in people's ethnicity, creed, religion, and way of thinking, and embraces all human hearts.

The peace that we human beings seek is built upon the dignity of our own life, and upon reverence for the lives of others. I urgently hope that now, each of us will grasp the opportunity to shed our feelings of selfishness and greed, and revive our lost spirit of humanitarian love, by joining hands in affirming the immenseness of our innate, sacred nature.

Is this not the best time for us to return to our starting point and create a way of life that will positively affect the lives of the next generation? Shall we not pass along to them a world filled with bright hopes for the future? Whether we do this or not depends on the choices that we make at the present moment.

Here, I would like to invite everyone to join in the Fuji Declaration—an affirmation of the dignity of our own lives and the awe that we feel in face of the lives of others. It was created as an expression of love and respect for the whole of humanity. It offers an opportunity for each of us to become a 'change-maker'—one who rekindles the divine spark in each human heart. In rekindling this divine spark, we can change negative thoughts, words, and actions into positive ones.

Bright, positive words are a creative power that springs from each human being's sublime, sacred consciousness—the consciousness of life itself. It is my belief that by exerting the power of light-filled words in our daily lives, we can unleash the momentum for creating a wondrous future on Earth.

Now is the time when we can make it happen. Starting right now, let us pass along no more negative words to future generations. Let our legacy include no more hostilities, no more wars, no more anger and greed, no more discrimination and conflict, no more poverty and starvation, no more illness. Let our legacy be one of un-limited human potential, dignity, respect, and love.

The decision is up to us.

May peace prevail on Earth.

The Fuji Declaration

Awakening the Divine Spark in the
Spirit of Humanity

**For a civilization of oneness with diversity on planet
earth**

A new phase in the evolution of human civilization is
on the horizon. With deepening states of crisis bringing
unrest to all parts of the world, there is a growing need
for change in our ways of thinking and acting. We now
have the choice of either spiraling into deepening peril,
or breaking through to a world of dignity and wellbeing
for all.

Throughout its history, humanity has been guided
primarily by a material consciousness. Fearing scarci-
ty, we have continued to pursue material gain beyond

necessity, taking from others and depleting the Earth's natural resources. If our aspirations continue to focus only on what is material and finite, our world will face inevitable destruction.

What is our true nature?

In order to make more enlightened choices and change the course of our history, we need to return to the basic question concerning human life. Each and every one of us must ask, "What is our true nature?" and seek a meaningful and responsible answer.

The great spiritual traditions of the world have always been telling us that, at its root, human life is inextricably linked to its universal source. Today, the latest advances in the physical and life sciences reaffirm this perennial insight. When we rediscover our connections to nature and the cosmos, we can re-align our life with the universal movement toward oneness and harmony in and through diversity. We can restore the divine spark in the human spirit and bring forth our innate love, compassion, wisdom, and joy to live a flourishing life. The time has come for every one of us to awaken the divine spark that resides in our heart.

What is the purpose of our existence?

We have been born at a critical juncture in history, in a world in transition, where it is possible to guide the advatncement of humankind toward peace on Earth. Living peace and enabling peace to prevail on Earth is the ultimate purpose for all of us. We can and must embrace it in every sphere of our existence.

By living consciously and responsibly, we can draw upon our inherent freedom and power to shape our destiny and the destiny of humankind. Our task is to collaboratively create a world of dignity and compassion that unfolds the full potential of the human spirit—a world in which every individual gives expression to his or her highest self, in service to the human family and the whole web of life on the planet.

Toward a new civilization

It is imperative to bring together individuals from diverse fields—scientists, artists, politicians, religious and business leaders, and others—to create a solid multidimensional foundation for catalyzing a timely shift in the course of history. The time has come for all people to become courageous pioneers—to venture beyond their personal, cultural, and national interests and beyond the boundaries of their discipline, and to come together in wisdom, spirit and intention for the benefit of all people in the human family. By so doing, we can overcome the hold of obsolete ideas and outdated behaviors in today's unsustainable world and design a more harmonious and flourishing civilization for the coming generations.

The paradigm of the new civilization

The paradigm of the new civilization is a culture of oneness with respect for diversity. Just as the myriad cells and diverse organs of our body are interconnected by their oneness and work together in harmony for the purpose of sustaining our life, so each and every living thing is an intrinsic part of the larger symphony of life on this planet. With the conscious recognition that we are all a part of a living universe consisting of great diversity yet embracing unity, we will co-evolve with one another and with nature through a network of constructive and coherent relationships.

We, as individuals responsible for our and our children's future, hereby declare that:

—We affirm the divine spark in the heart and mind of every human being and intend to live by its light in every sphere of our existence.

—We commit ourselves to fulfilling our shared mission of creating lasting peace on Earth through our ways of living and acting.

—We intend to live and act so as to enhance the quality of life and the well-being of all forms of life on the planet, recognizing that all living things in all their diversity are interconnected and are one.

—We continually and consistently strive to free the human spirit for deep creativity, and to nurture the necessary transformation to forge a new paradigm in all spheres of human activity, including economics, science, medicine, politics, business, education, religion, the arts, communications and the media.

—We shall make it our mission to design, communicate and implement a more spiritual and harmonious civilization—a civilization that enables humankind to realize its inherent potential and advance to the next stage of its material, spiritual, and cultural evolution.

*To sign the declaration, please go to **fujideclaration.org**.*

*Note: In May 2016, the Soul of WoMen campaign was inaugurated as a project of The Fuji Declaration. For information, please visit **fujideclaration.org/soulofwomen**.*

We Are Making It Happen

Message from Masami Saionji to the 4.27 DMZ International Peace Conference in Cheorwon, South Korea

It is a great pleasure for me to be here with all of you in this history-making 'Hand-in-Hand' celebration at the DMZ between North and South Korea.

I would like to express my heartfelt gratitude to Dr. Peter Jiseok Jung—who has devoted himself heart and soul to preparing for this day—and to each and every one of you who have come together to be part of this very special moment.

It is no coincidence that you have been able to gather here today. For a long time, you have been thinking about just one thing: 'How can I be of service to others? How can I help safeguard the earth and all living things? What can I do to help create a better neighborhood, a better country, and a better world?'

For a long time, this heart's desire has been burning within you, suppressed by feelings of separation and a lack of self-confidence.

But now, the time has come when this inner, peace-loving instinct—this divine spark of all human beings—is about to come alive again. And each one of you stands at the forefront of this brilliant transformation.

We must free ourselves from the mistaken thought that some outside force or situation can control us. All lives are equal and valuable. All lives are sacred and born free. No matter what our skin color is, no matter what background we have, we all have the power to make our own choices, and change the course of humanity's future.

Today's celebration will touch the hearts of people all over the world. This 'Hand-in-Hand' event is the first step in a large-scale transformation.

Thanks to your presence here today, peace will come to North and South Korea. It will happen. We are making it happen. The time for peace has come.

Thank you very much. *May peace prevail on Earth.*

(Delivered by Masami Saionji at the
Hand-in-Hand dinner reception on April 26, 2019)

Invitation to Fuji Sanctuary

Message from Masami Saionji to the 2019 "Great Gathering to Help Mother Earth" held in Bad Blumau, Austria

Honorable Oyaté-tha-Tacan'sina, distinguished elders, brothers and sisters, peace workers and guests,

I feel tremendously privileged to have been invited to join in this "Help Mother Earth" Great Gathering held from July 3-7. As soon as I received the moving letter of invitation from Oyaté-tha-Tacan'sina I was determined to come. However, I soon realized that because of our own Great Gathering, also set for July 7, I would not be able to attend in person. And so, from Japan, I would like to offer my heartfelt greetings and sentiments of deep respect.

As Tacan'sina has explained, if we wish to help Mother Earth, we currently can have the greatest impact through peace ceremonies and prayers. Here in Japan, our world peace prayer ceremonies are centered at a place called Fuji Sanctuary, located in the foothills of sacred Mount Fuji. I would like to invite all of you to come and visit this high-dimensional place, and experience how it feels to sit in the prayer field, encircled by the flags of all nations and regions on Earth.

Day in and day out, for more than 20 years, these national flags have been waving high in the air at Fuji Sanctuary, infusing the land with the pure spirit of their nations' people.

Once a month, in all kinds of weather, peace-loving people travel to Fuji Sanctuary from all over Japan and the world to sit in the presence of sacred Mount Fuji. There, they join together in heartfelt prayers for peace on Earth and the divine re-awakening of the human consciousness.

And once a year, Fuji Sanctuary welcomes leaders from all the world's religions and spiritual traditions, who lead us in praying their own chosen prayers—creating a great Symphony of Peace Prayers. In the wind, in the rain, in the snow, and under the noonday sun, some 10,000 people join together in praying these peace prayers. They also pray in the national languages of each country for peace to prevail in each nation on Earth.

This spirit of heartfelt prayer, this peace-filled consciousness, spreads out from Fuji Sanctuary to all people in all lands, re-enlivening the innate divine spark in each human heart.

From the bottom of my heart I would like to thank each one of you for your divine awareness, and your deep dedication to helping Mother Earth. With the power of our prayerful consciousness, we can spark a divine reawakening in all human beings. One by one, all of humanity will wake up and apologize to Mother Earth for our past, shameful behavior.

We have the power to change the world if we take it step by step. Step by step, we can inspire ourselves and others to change our way of thinking. Step by step, our prayerful way of living will have a positive influence on others, until all people find themselves naturally loving the earth, respecting the earth, and healing the earth with the vibrations of their deep gratitude.

Once again I thank you from the bottom of my heart for your earnest dedication to Mother Earth.

May Peace Prevail on Earth,
Masami Saionji

*Oyaté-tha-Tacan'sina is a Wicasa Pezuta (Medicine Man) and the founder of Canglesa Takata (**www.canglesa-takata.world**). To learn more about the Great Gathering "Help Mother Earth," please visit **www.hilf-mutter-erde.de/english** or **facebook.com/Vision.der.neuen.Zeit**.*

About the Author

Descended from the Royal Ryuku Family of Okinawa, Masami Saionji was born in Tokyo, Japan. She was educated in Japan at Gakushuin Women's Junior College and studied English in the United States at Michigan State and Stanford Universities. At an early age, she became a Master of Japanese Classical Dance, and taught students for more than ten years.

While in her teens, she came in touch with the peace vision of philosopher Masahisa Goi, who later designated her as his successor and adopted daughter. She now heads several peace organizations, including the Goi Peace Foundation, founded in Japan, and May Peace Prevail on Earth International, headquartered in New York. She is perhaps best known for her leadership of the international Peace Pole Initiative, which places visual reminders of peace in key locations around the world.

In November 2001, Ms. Saionji was named an honorary member of the Club of Budapest in recognition of her exceptional efforts for world peace. She is the recipient of the Philosopher Saint Shree Dnyaneshwara World Peace Prize (2008), the WON Award honoring distinguished women leaders (2010), the Dr. Barbara Fields Humanitarian Peace Award (2016), and the Luxembourg Peace Prize (2019).

In February 2013, she had the privilege of presenting the Symphony of Peace Prayers ceremony at the United Nations, in a special event entitled *United for a Culture of Peace through Interfaith Harmony*, which was hosted by the president of the UN General Assembly. In 2015, she initiated the Fuji Declaration along with her husband Hiroo and Dr. Ervin Laszlo.

Masami Saionji has authored over twenty books in Japanese and twelve in English and other languages. She has lived in North America and Europe, and travels extensively on speaking and seminar tours. She and her husband, the descendant of a Japanese prime minister, have three daughters. They currently live in Tokyo.

The author welcomes your comments, impressions, or experiences concerning this book. Please send them to:

Masami Saionji – English Publications
Hitoana 812-1
Fujinomiya, Japan 418-0102
E-mail: info@thinksomethingwonderful.net

Internet users are invited to visit:

www.goipeace.or.jp
www.worldpeace.org
www.fujideclaration.org
www.thinksomethingwonderful.net
www.earthhealershandbook.net

65840176R00119

Made in the USA
Middletown, DE
09 September 2019